WASHINGTON
Off the Beaten Path

Also by Todd Litman and Suzanne Kort

The Best Bike Rides in the Pacific Northwest

WASHINGTON
Off the Beaten Path™

by

Todd Litman
and Suzanne Kort

A Voyager Book

The Globe Pequot Press

Old Saybrook, Connecticut

Off the Beaten Path is a trademark of The Globe Pequot Press, Inc.

Library of Congress Cataloging-in-Publication Data

Litman, Todd
   Washington : off the beaten path / by Todd Litman and Suzanne Kort. — 1st ed.
      p.   cm.
   "A Voyager book."
   Includes index.
   ISBN 1-56440-140-5
   1. Washington (State)—Guidebooks.   I. Kort, Suzanne.
II. Title
F889.3.L58 1993
917.9704'43—dc20   92-42524
                                        CIP

Cover: The Perkins House, Colfax

Manufactured in the United States of America
First Edition/First Printing

This book is dedicated to
Norma Riva Litman*, 1929–1992,*
whose spirit of adventure, curiosity, and service
is an inspiration to all whose lives she touched;
*and to our predecessor, **Stephen Graham,** 1884–1975,*
who wrote The Gentle Art of Tramping.

Acknowledgments

We would like to express our appreciation to the many people who shared suggestions, assistance, and hospitality in the development of this book. Special thanks to Russ Cahill, Karen Farber, Greg and Laura Ware, and Michael and Karen Huntsburger of Olympia; Dennis Conner of Lynden; Terri Gravelle and Paul Mathews of Oakesdale; Mary Leitka of the Hoh Reservation; Nick and Donna Manring of Garfield; Virginia Miller of Republic; Kay Ritchie and Dennis Conomos of Forks; and Margaret, Dorothy, and David Watson of Spokane. The book was also enriched by staff members of numerous visitors bureaus and public agencies, who reviewed our work to ensure its accuracy. We extend warm thanks to Beverley, Shirley, and Sol Kort of Vancouver, B.C., for their help with our Okanogan and Stehekin explorations; Norma and Marshall Litman of Davis, California, for their delightful assistance exploring Whidbey Island; Graham and Raviv Kort Litman for contributing so much to our adventures; and Michael Sell for looking after the home front during our trips across Washington.

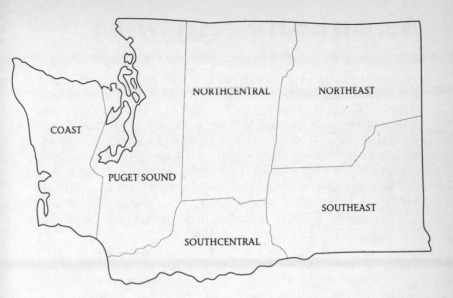

Contents

About the Authors

Suzanne Kort and Todd Litman are seasoned travelers with a penchant for the unusual and a love of writing. A native of Vancouver, B.C., Suzanne developed an early appreciation for forest environments and a tolerance for maritime climates. Her travels through Europe, the Mideast, China, the Caribbean, and North America, and living within Native American communities, impressed her with a respect for cultural and environmental diversity. She has translated her impressions into journals and poetry, some of which have appeared in regional publications, radio programs, and live readings. Suzanne is a full-time parent with a degree in environmental studies.

During his younger days Todd traveled extensively through Mexico, Europe, and South America. Since settling in Washington state he has explored Puget Sound in small, traditional boats and by bicycle. Todd has published numerous articles on bicycling and transportation policy. He works as an Energy Specialist for Washington State and is completing his master's degree in environmental policy. Suzanne and Todd are married and live with their two sons, Graham and Raviv, in a turn-of-the-century farmhouse in Olympia, Washington. In addition to *Washington: Off the Beaten Path*, Todd and Suzanne co-authored *The Best Bike Rides in the Pacific Northwest*, also published by The Globe Pequot Press.

Introduction

Washington is a generous state, offering something for everyone. You'll find dense evergreen forests, fertile farmlands, dynamic cities, and foggy islands. There are many well-known tourist destinations, but the real fun begins when you explore off the beaten path. Poke around in Washington and you might find a secluded, windblown beach where you can watch whales, explore tide pools, or just absorb the fresh salt air (Shi-Shi, Ruby, Waikiki, and Klipsan beaches in chapter 1); a friendly small-town cafe where hard-working local folk welcome visitors with a smile and a story (Wacaunda in chapter 3 and the town of Palouse in chapter 6); a charming village, accessible only by boat or plane, nestled between a crystal-clear lake and a rugged mountain wilderness (Stehekin in chapter 3); or a hilltop mansion now renovated into a reasonably priced bed and breakfast where visitors enjoy personal hospitality and great food (Oakesdale's Hanford Castle in chapter 6).

Off the beaten path you'll discover unexpected delights, a slower pace, and relatively low costs for food and lodging. There are many special places that are not well known, even among longtime state residents. You'll find authentic, friendly communities, many with unique historical, environmental, or educational attractions. These are not novelty attractions, included just because they are cute or unusual. We chose destinations we think you will consider enjoyable, rewarding, and personally meaningful. From dramatic geologic formations to friendly bed and breakfast inns, these are places that we hope will renew your sense of wonder and will send you home with a richer appreciation for this land we call Washington.

This book is not for everybody. If you prefer common tourist activities, want predictable experiences, or are uncomfortable meeting people in their own environment, you may as well put this book down. We've written this guide to help adventurous spirits find some of Washington's best places that might otherwise be overlooked. Some of these destinations are moderately well known, especially in their part of the state, while others are true finds that deserve more attention than they currently receive.

One reviewer, after reading a section of this book, advised us to devote fewer words to each destination so we could squeeze more in. We ignored this recommendation; there already are plenty of guides that provide quantity without identifying quality. Rather than give so many suggestions that you'd have to hurry to see them all, we've highlighted a few that we think are especially good. We believe that the biggest mistake you could make is to rush as you travel, missing the subtleties of this special land.

Many of the communities described in this book are experiencing a revival. New cultural events, civic organizations, and innovative businesses in several of the smaller towns reflect residents' renewed hope and pride. There are numerous efforts to preserve the state's unique environment and heritage for visitors and future generations. As you travel around the state, you'll find many opportunities to share in this excitement.

If we can explore Washington, so can you. We traveled thousands of miles over highways and back roads researching this book. We often got lost, which sometimes resulted in our discovering yet another delightful but little-known attraction. Most trips were made in a funky old VW camper, with our three-year-old son, Graham, setting the pace. Our second son, Raviv, was born during the final days of this project.

The routes described here are mainly on paved roads, and you are seldom far from a town. If in doubt about your next destination, carry a stock of snacks so you can stop for a picnic at some idyllic location. A small portable cooler is handy. The weather in Washington is unpredictable, even in summer, so always be prepared for a change. A well-adapted Washingtonian is never discouraged by a little rain.

This book, a state road map, and a sense of adventure are the basic tools you need to travel around Washington off the beaten path. We've provided a list, at the back of the book, of resources and organizations that can offer additional help exploring this intriguing state. If you have comments about this book or suggestions for future editions, please contact us in care of The Globe Pequot Press, P.O. Box 833, Old Saybrook, CT 06475-0833.

Thumbnail Sketch of Washington State

Washington is part of the Pacific Northwest, which also includes Southeast Alaska, British Columbia, Idaho, Western Montana, and Oregon. The state is divided by the Cascade Mountains into eastern and western regions. This division is climatic, economic, and social. The western side has lots of rain, industry, and people. The eastern side of the state is relatively dry, agricultural, and rural.

Western Washington has hundreds of miles of dramatic and beautiful coastline. To the north is the Olympic Peninsula, to the south are forest-covered hills and the mouth of the great Columbia River. Puget Sound's inland waters lap the shores of countless bays and islands. The San Juan Islands sit like jewels in the Strait of Juan de Fuca. Along the mainland are thick forests and rich farmlands. Urban growth along the Interstate 5 corridor is encroaching on much of this open land, replacing small, rural communities with busy cities.

Stretches of the Interstate 5 corridor are as populated with sprawling suburbs as Southern California. Seattle, the Emerald City, is a hot spot of business and culture. Scattered along the Sound are smaller cities and towns, some known for industry, others as retirement and art communities. A few areas around the Sound are still relatively undeveloped, especially the western side and some of the less-accessible islands, but all are suffering from pressures associated with growth. There is almost universal agreement among Puget Sound residents that the special amenities of this region should be preserved, although there is great debate over how that goal should be accomplished.

Western Washington is covered with timber "thick as hair on the back of a dog." Timber harvesting and processing, a primary industry in much of rural Washington, is facing hard times as increasing demands are placed on limited resources. It's a challenging time for many families and small communities who are proud of their rich and industrious past.

Washington is famous for its magnificent mountains, including several volcanoes, the Olympic Mountains in the northwest, the Selkirk Range in the northeast, the Blue Mountains to the southeast, and the towering Cascades running through the center of the state. There are five passes over the Cascade Mountains. Because of difficult weather and heavy snowpack, only three are open year-round. The mountains offer something for all tastes: challenging peaks for hard-core climbers, ski resorts with runs catering to all levels of skill, gentle nature trails through old-growth forests, and numerous retreats along pristine alpine lakes. Many Washington residents become connoisseurs of mountain environments, developing a sophisticated appreciation of their geology, natural history, and aesthetics.

Eastern Washington has dry summers and cold winters. The landscape is a mixture of wheat-covered hills, dry scrublands, ancient river canyons (called coulees), and aromatic pine forests. While western Washington grows increasingly urban and experiences problems of rapid growth, eastern Washington has only a few scattered cities and many small towns, some of which have experienced declining populations in recent years.

Native residents have lived in the land that is now Washington state for thousands of years, but European culture is relatively recent. Few Washington towns were established before 1850, but a lot has happened in the past century and a half. Many towns are working to preserve their heritage in local museums, renovated buildings, and by painting historical murals. In most communities you'll have no trouble finding old-timers who are delighted to describe the days when Washington was a frontier state.

The early days were not easy for either natives or immigrants. Epidemics, the Indian Wars of the 1850s, and increasingly restrictive treaties destroyed much of the native culture. Indian tribes are now working especially hard to preserve their traditional culture and legends. Several tribes have created outstanding museums, some highlighted in this book, where both tribal members and visitors can learn about the land's first people.

Off the Beaten Path on the Washington Coast

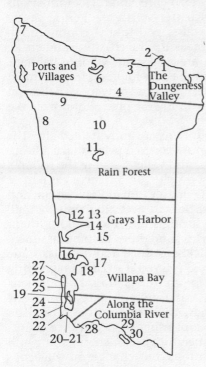

Ports and Villages

The Dungeness Valley

Rain Forest

Grays Harbor

Willapa Bay

Along the Columbia River

10. Hoh River Visitor Center and Nature Trail
11. Lochaerie Resort
12. Hoquiam Castle
13. Aberdeen Museum of History
14. Grays Harbor Historical Seaport
15. Clark's Ice Cream Shoppe
16. Tokeland Hotel & Restaurant
17. Dennis Company
18. Pacific County Historical Museum
19. Willapa National Wildlife Refuge
20. Ilwaco Heritage Museum
21. Inn at Ilwaco
22. Cape Disappointment Interpretive Center
23. Shelburne Country Inn and Shoalwater Restaurant
24. World Kite Museum and Hall of Fame
25. Ark Restaurant and Bakery
26. Oysterville
27. Leadbetter Point State Park
28. Sanctuary Restaurant
29. Columbia White-tailed Deer National Wildlife Refuge
30. Wahkiakum County Historical Museum

1. Groveland Cottage Bed and Breakfast Inn
2. Dungeness National Wildlife Refuge
3. Arthur D. Feiro Marine Laboratory
4. Hurricane Ridge
5. Log Cabin Resort
6. Lake Crescent Lodge
7. Makah Museum
8. Manitou Lodge
9. Miller Tree Inn

Washington Coast

Washington's Pacific Ocean coastline stretches from the Strait of Juan de Fuca to the north to the mouth of the Columbia River to the south. It's a land of contrasts. The Olympic Peninsula's ocean shoreline is rugged, with steep cliffs and rocky formations sculpted by wave and wind. Farther south are gentle sandy beaches lined with summer cottages and tourist communities. Grays Harbor and Willapa Bay break up the coastline and create extensive inland wetlands that are important wildlife habitats. The Olympic Peninsula rain forest has the highest annual rainfall on the continental United States, yet the Dungeness Valley on the Strait of Juan de Fuca has the lowest precipitation on the coast north of California.

The magnificent Olympic Mountains are aptly named after the home of the Greek gods; their snow-covered peaks make a beautiful backdrop to beaches, forests, and valleys, giving the region a mystical quality. The outer coast beaches are protected as part of the Olympic National Park and Quinault Indian Reservation, and road access is limited. Several beaches are accessible only by trail, and some stretches disappear during high tide, making them treacherous for careless hikers who sometimes become stranded.

Most of the coast region is thickly forested and includes some of the world's largest living trees, yet you'll need a magnifying lens to appreciate the details of the countless mosses and lichens that help create this distinctive environment. Except for a few larger towns and tourist beaches, the communities along the coast are dependent on timber and other basic resource industries. Many local families have been loggers, fishermen, or mill workers for three or four generations, but changes in the economy are forcing many individuals, businesses, and communities to rethink their goals and identity. Despite the changes, coastal communities retain their rich pioneer and aboriginal cultures. These are not just historical traditions; they continue to evolve. Loggers now use their chain-saw skills to make sculpture, and invitations to Indian potlatch ceremonies are often faxed between native tribes.

Visitors to coastal communities have lots to see and do. You can visit local historical museums, contemplate the coast's exquisite beauty from a secluded beach, learn about the region's unique natural environment, or join the carnival fun of a busy beachside tourist resort. There are numerous outdoor activities to enjoy: hiking, bicycling, fishing, birding, and beachcombing. Be sure to bring rain gear and good walking shoes or boots so you can take advantage of the many trails and beaches and become intimate with this unique environment.

The Dungeness Valley

The Olympic Mountains' towering peaks shelter this picturesque valley from the copious rainfall of the Pacific Northwest, making it famous as the "banana belt" of the Northwest coast. The valley's traditional economy was based on farming, fishing, and logging. Farming with only 14 inches of annual rainfall requires irrigation, and the community has celebrated its good fortunes with an Irrigation Festival the beginning of each May since 1896. Activities include tours of the Dungeness River irrigation system and the farms that rely on it, a mile-long Grand Parade, old-fashioned salmon bakes, as well as displays of art, logging, and natural history. Festival information is available from the Sequim Visitor Information Center, 1192 East Washington Street, (206) 683–6197, open 9:00 A.M. to 5:00 P.M. daily.

The town of **Sequim** (pronounced skwim) is the commercial center of the Dungeness Valley and a good base from which to explore the valley's highlights, despite the "strip" development of the town's main street. There are plenty of guest houses in the area. For seclusion you can choose the quiet **Diamond Point Inn** (241 Sunshine Road, Sequim 98382; 800–551–2615) or the hilltop **Greywolf Inn** (177 Keeler Road, Sequim 98382; 206–683–5889), both of which offer hospitality in rural settings outside of town. Families will appreciate **Granny Sandy's Orchard Inn** (405 West Spruce, Sequim 98382; 800–841–3347) for a homey atmosphere. As her nickname indicates, Granny Sandy dotes on children. **Casoni's,** a Mom and Pop-style restaurant located at Highway 101 and Carlsborg Junction, offers Italian and continental cuisine from 4:00 to 9:00 P.M. daily in summer, Wednesday through Sunday from Labor Day to mid-May. Call (206) 683–2415 for reservations.

Just west of the Sequim city limits at the end of Hendrickson Road is the **Dungeness River Railroad Bridge Park,** a beautiful park that includes nature trails down to the river and the

Olympic Peninsula Natural History Museum Interpretive Center (610 North Fifth Avenue), where you can become acquainted with this region's unique wildlife, plants, and intertidal life through colorful dioramas and exhibits. Take Taylor Cut-off Road south from Highway 101 toward the mountains to reach **Lost Mountain Winery,** 3142 Lost Mountain Road. Call (206) 683–5229 to arrange a review of Romeo Conca's delicious red dinner wines. Also in the hills above Sequim you'll find **Cedarbrook Herb Farm** (986 South Sequim Avenue; 206–683–7733), a twelve-acre farm planted in aromatic herbs and native plants. At the farm's 100-year-old Bell House, you can purchase dried herbs, herb vinegars, dried flower bouquets and wreaths, garlic ropes, and herb sachets. Visitors are welcome to stroll through the gardens, which include views over the town to the Strait of Juan de Fuca and the San Juan Islands.

To explore the historic community of **Dungeness,** head north from Highway 101 on Sequim-Dungeness Way in downtown Sequim. Dungeness is old by Washington state standards, named in 1792 by British explorer Captain George Vancouver for a cape on England's south coast. Early settlers found the Dungeness River Valley rich with resources and accessible for shipping lumber, and agricultural and dairy products as far as San Francisco. Charles Seal established The Dungeness Trading Company in the 1890s and built a mansion with the proceeds. Simone Nichols recently renovated Seal's charming country mansion into ⊃**Groveland Cottage Bed and Breakfast Inn** (4861 Sequim-Dungeness Way, Dungeness 98382; 206–683–3565). Guests wake up to beautiful views of mountains, gardens, and the sea. The gracious staff pampers guests with a morning paper and their favorite hot beverage at their bedroom door before a delicious breakfast served in the dining room. The inn also includes a gallery and general store that features the works of local artists, a selection of fine wines, coffees, and treats, as well as groceries. Older children only are allowed at the inn.

The sleepy town of Dungeness is a pleasant place to explore. You'll see the historic **Dungeness Schoolhouse,** built in 1892 and used to educate local children until 1955, as well as several turn-of-the-century homes amidst fields, creeks, and wetlands. **Skyline Nursery** features rare perennials, wildflowers, alpine plants, and native Washington plants. Dennis Doran's **Dungeness Chainsaw Carvings Shop** (4970 Sequim-Dungeness Way,

Dungeness 98382; 206–683–2597) overflows with an impressive and often humorous array of wood sculptures. Dungeness Road ends at the ever-popular **Three Crabs Restaurant,** known for its seafood specialties such as Dungeness cracked crab, smoked salmon, oysters supreme, almond red snapper, and halibut. After your meal you may want to stroll down the beach toward Cline Spit, or simply sit on a driftwood log and watch ship traffic through the strait. The restaurant is open daily for lunch and dinner. Call (206) 683–4264 early for reservations; this busy spot fills up fast.

A fun place to visit near Dungeness is the **Olympic Game Farm,** 1423 Ward Road. Guided walking tours in summer or drive-through tours year-round will put you in the company of four-legged stars. Walt Disney Studios has employed farm residents, including grizzlies and wolves, in more than eighty wildlife productions. Many animals you'll see there, from Siberian tigers and African lions to North American timber wolves and bison, are on the endangered species list. Snacks are available for you as well as for the animals. The game farm opens daily at 9:00 A.M. from June 1 through October 1 and at 10:00 A.M. from October 2 through May 31. Call (206) 683–4295 for closing times.

The ☼**Dungeness National Wildlife Refuge,** located northwest of the game farm, offers an exhilarating immersion in an uncaged wilderness. You can take an easy quarter-mile hike to a viewpoint overlooking **Dungeness Spit,** one of the nation's largest natural sand hooks. Dungeness Spit is one of the last major stands of undisturbed eelgrass beds in Puget Sound, making it a much-beloved feeding ground for black brant geese that depend on these water-loving grasses for food. You may see blubbery heaps of harbor seals hauled out at the end of the spit or perhaps just their playful heads bobbing about as they fish and frolic offshore. Spring and fall are the best times to visit, when thousands of water birds make their annual migrations. You can follow the 6-mile trail through the forest and down the beach to the end of the spit. On the west side, you'll experience the roar of incoming waves; on the east, the quiet of a sheltered bay. At the end of the spit, you'll find the **New Dungeness Lighthouse.** Built in 1857 and automated in 1937, this is the oldest lighthouse north of the Columbia River. For more information, write Washington Coastal Refuges Office, 33 South Barr Road, Port Angeles 98362, or call (206) 457–8451.

The best way to go through the Dungeness Valley between Sequim and Port Angeles is on the **Old Olympic Highway.** This pleasant, less traveled route through green farmlands gives you magnificent views of the mountains rising to the south. For a different perspective, turn south on Deer Park Road (3 miles east of Port Angeles) for a winding 19-mile climb over the forest-covered slopes of Blue Mountain to **Deer Park** in Olympic National Park. Here you'll find an alpine campground and ranger station (open in summer only) and the trailhead to magnificent day hikes overlooking the Dungeness Valley, Port Angeles, and the Strait of Juan de Fuca.

Ports and Villages

Port Angeles, the largest city on the Olympic Peninsula, is dominated by its busy waterfront. This deep-water harbor is a port of call for international shipping, a center of ocean fishing, a major Coast Guard Station, and terminus for Black Ball's *Coho* ferry, which makes daily trips to Victoria, B.C. The City Pier, one block east of the ferry terminal, is a good starting point for your explorations. There you'll find a small park, a four-story-high viewing tower, a berth for the 210-foot Coast Guard cutter *Active,* a public marine laboratory, and plenty of nearby restaurants and shops. The ⊃**Arthur D. Feiro Marine Laboratory** located on the Pier is the place to see and even touch the remarkable sea creatures that live on Washington's coast. You can watch the graceful movements of an octopus, stroke a stuffed sea lion, and handle a variety of living marine animals in the touch-tanks. Docents answer questions and describe in nontechnical language the Northwest region's marine ecology. The laboratory is open for a small admission fee from 10:00 A.M. to 8:00 P.M. daily from mid-June to Labor Day, and from noon to 4:00 P.M. on weekends the rest of the year. For more information call (206) 452–9277, extension 264.

There is lots to explore along the Port Angeles waterfront. You can pick up a walking tour brochure at the Visitors Center (located next to the City Pier), which describes historic highlights. The Waterfront Trail, which follows the harbor shore east along Hollywood Beach, is ideal for walking or bicycling. You can also bicycle west to **Ediz Hook,** the natural sand spit that forms the Port Angeles harbor. Bikes are available for rent at **Pedal 'n Pack** (120 East Front Street; 206–457–1240). At the end of the hook is the U.S. Coast Guard Air Station. Bicycle or drive along the 4-mile spit for spectacular views of the Strait of Juan de Fuca to the north and the city with the Olympic Mountains as a backdrop to the south. To reach the hook, follow Marine Drive west through the Daishowa America paper mill. Along the spit are six picnic sites with windbreaks, rest rooms, and handicapped access. If you enjoy watching the waterfront activities, you'll want to stay at **Baytons' on the Bluff Bed and Breakfast** (824 West Fourth Street, Port Angeles 98362; 206–457–5569), a large, comfortable bed-and-breakfast home that offers panoramic views of the harbor, the strait, and Vancouver Island beyond. Or you may prefer the historic **Kennedy's** (332 East Fifth Street, Port Angeles 98362; 206–457–3628), located just a few blocks from the Victoria ferry terminal. This 1896 home was recently refurbished with modern comforts yet retains its turn-of-the-century charm.

⊃**Hurricane Ridge** is accessible by an 18-mile paved road from Port Angeles. It's a spectacular area to explore, offering panoramic views of the Strait of Juan de Fuca and islands to the north, and the alpine meadows and glacier-covered peaks of the Olympic Mountains to the south. National Park rangers lead walks and answer visitors' questions. You can choose from several hikes through the area's meadows and rocky ridge. The Hurricane Ridge Lodge, open 10:00 A.M. to 5:00 P.M. during the summer and winter seasons, includes a museum, deli, and gift shop. Rest rooms are open year-round. For more information stop by the Olympic National Park Visitors Center at the south end of Race Street in Port Angeles, open daily from 8:30 A.M. to 5:30 P.M. July 1 through September 30, and 9:00 A.M. to 4:00 P.M. October 1 through June 30, or call (206) 452–0330.

Nine miles west of Port Angeles, you can turn south on Olympic Hot Springs Road to explore the beautiful **Elwha River Valley.** The Press Expedition, one of the first groups to explore and map the heart of the Olympic Mountains, followed this route. Although the lower portion of the river is now dammed, there is still much to see. Stop at the Elwha Ranger Station for information on hiking trails and the Olympic Hot Springs, or take a raft trip down the scenic Elwha River. Contact the **Olympic Raft and Guide Service** (c/o Elwha Resort, 464

Highway 101 West, Port Angeles 98362; 206–457–7011), which runs daily morning and afternoon trips.

West of Port Angeles, you can either follow Highway 101 inland or take Highway 112 along the coastline. If you opt for the inland route, you'll find a beautiful destination at **Lake Crescent,** a shimmering azure blue jewel set in the emerald green of surrounding forests. It's a large lake, 10 miles long and more than a mile wide. Much of the area around the lake is preserved as part of the Olympic National Forest. A right turn onto East Beach Road at Lake Crescent's eastern edge will take you along a scenic, winding lakeside road to the ɔ**Log Cabin Resort** (6549 East Beach Road, Port Angeles 98362; 206–928–3325). Established in 1895 on the lake's isolated north shore, the "sunny side of the lake," the resort's unpretentious cabins, general store, and restaurant provide a secluded, friendly atmosphere. Guests can rent rowboats or canoes to enjoy fishing or relaxing on the lake. You can hike among giant old-growth cedars and firs or rent mountain bikes to explore forest trails. The 4-mile Spruce Division Railroad Trail, originally a railroad grade built during World War I to help extract spruce logs for airplane production, is a great way to experience the lake's north shore.

A visitor information center is located on the lake's south shore just off Highway 101 in a log cabin built in 1905 by Olympic Forest ranger Chris Morgenroth. From the cabin a three-quarter-mile trail follows a level, gravel path through the forest that ends with an uphill climb to the 90-foot **Marymere Falls,** offering visitors a pleasant excursion through this rain-forest wonderland. The ɔ**Lake Crescent Lodge** (H.C. 62, Box 11, Port Angeles 98362; 206–928–3211), just west of the visitor center, is a classic, elegant resort that has changed little since it was built on the lakeshore in 1915. It was while staying here in 1937 that President Franklin Roosevelt decided to create Olympic National Park in order to preserve this area's beauty for future generations. Visitors enjoy boating, fishing, and nature hikes, in addition to lounging under the shade of a lakeside tree. In the resort restaurant you can watch the sun set over the lake while savoring a fine dinner.

The **Olympic Park Institute,** located nearby at the historic **Rosemary Inn,** offers programs for children and adults on subjects ranging from creative writing to natural history and environmental ethics. The rustic resort, established on Lake Crescent

Lake Crescent Lodge Sun Room

in 1914, is considered an outstanding example of the "Craftsman Era" of American architecture. For a calendar of upcoming classes, write the Olympic Park Institute, HC 62, Box 9T, Port Angeles 98362, or call (206) 928–3720.

You'll find forested campgrounds, boat rentals, and groceries at Fairholm on the western edge of Lake Crescent. A 12-mile drive up Sol Duc Road takes you to **Sol Duc Hot Springs Resort** (P.O. Box 2169, Port Angeles 98362; 206–327–3583). Sol Duc (also written Soleduck) means "sparkling water" in the Quileute language. Visitors have been flocking to the healthy mineral waters at Sol Duc since a magnificent spa was first built at the site in 1912 (and, sadly, burned in 1916). The new resort, open mid-May through the last full week of September, offers three large outdoor hot mineral pools, elegant dining, and cabins. Camping, hiking trails, and naturalist programs are available nearby at the **Sol Duc Olympic National Park** campground.

Take the Highway 112 turnoff at the junction west of Port Angeles if you want magnificent views of the Olympic Peninsula's rugged northern coastline. Ten miles west of Port Angeles, turn north on Camp Hayden Road to reach **Salt Creek Recreation Area** (206–928–3441), a marine sanctuary with tide pools full of waving sea anemones, gooseneck barnacles, coal-black mussels, and colorful starfish, as well as kelp beds and rocky islands offshore. Continuing west on Highway 112, you may see a gray whale spouting offshore, or perhaps a pod of orca or a California sea lion swimming by. Watch for crowds of harbor seals relaxing on the tiny islands offshore.

Continue west to Neah Bay or take the turnoff on Hoko-Ozette Road, just past the fishing village of Sekiu on Clallam Bay, to **Lake Ozette.** The lake, which is the largest natural body of fresh water in Washington state, is a great place to paddle a canoe or rowboat. By boat you can explore miles of wild shoreline and secluded campsites not accessible by land. The 10-mile loop trail around the lake to the coast makes a long day hike or you can stay overnight at secluded coastal campsites. The ranger station at Ozette can provide tide tables and other important information before you head off on these potentially dangerous beach trails. The park offers interpretive programs in the summer as well as a pleasant twenty-two-site campground at the lake's north end.

For an easy day hike from Ozette, walk along the 3-mile boardwalk over coastal wetlands to beautiful Cape Alava, the site of an ancient Makah Indian fishing village that was buried by a mud slide 500 years ago and recently excavated. The well-preserved contents of the village, exposed by tidal action in the 1970s, are housed at the ꓛ**Makah Museum,** which is part of the Makah Cultural and Research Center in Neah Bay, on the Makah Indian Reservation located 16 miles due north (but over 40 miles by road). This magnificent museum, owned and operated by the Makah Tribe, tells the story of people who lived a rigorous life hunting whales, seals, and fish, as well as creating beautiful works of art. The museum craft shop, and other shops in town, displays the work of Neah Bay's resident Makah artists. The museum, which charges a small entrance fee, is open from 10:00 A.M. to 5:00 P.M. daily in summer, and Wednesday through Sunday from mid-September to the end of May. For more information write to the museum at P.O. Box 95, Neah Bay 98357, or call (206) 645–2711.

Neah Bay is also the site of the annual Makah Days celebration, held the last weekend in August, which features traditional dancing and singing, salmon bakes, and canoe races. The **Thunderbird Resort,** on the waterfront, has kitchen and sleeping units, boat moorage, and booking information on charters for halibut, bottom fish, and salmon. Contact the resort office at P.O. Box 193, Neah Bay 98357, or call (206) 645–2450. Neah Bay's waterfront is crowded with commercial and private fishing boats. If you don't enjoy fishing, you can go out to watch whales, sea lions, and other abundant marine wildlife.

Follow signs to the Makah Air Force Station west of Neah Bay and take the right-hand fork to reach a rugged half-mile trail to **Cape Flattery,** the northwesternmost point in the contiguous United States. This rocky point has great views of Tatoosh Island, a half-mile-long volcanic outcropping that was once a favorite Makah retreat and is now home to a century-old lighthouse and nesting sea birds. This is a good place to get a close-up view of gray whales, which are often sighted feeding in the area during their annual migrations up the coast from May through June. Cape Flattery gets an average of 215 days of precipitation a year, so bring rain gear and good boots.

To reach breathtaking ocean beaches, take the south fork at the Air Force Station. **Hobuck, Sooes,** and **Shi-Shi beaches** are all located on the outer coast a few miles south of Neah Bay. From Makkaw Bay south the beaches are spectacular and unspoiled. Shi-Shi (shy-shy) Beach is accessible only by a 3-mile hike south of Sooes Beach. The **Makah National Fish Hatchery,** located on a dirt road just south of Sooes Beach, is open daily year-round and welcomes visitors to its salmon-spawning facilities. When you're ready to continue your peninsula journey, return east on Highway 112 and take the turnoff south on Burnt Mountain Road, located 6 miles south of Clallam Bay, back to Highway 101.

Rain Forest

Burnt Mountain Road connects to Highway 101 at Sappho. A mile farther west you can take Pavel Road 2 miles to the **Solduc Salmon Hatchery.** The hatchery has a small interpretive center with colorful dioramas illustrating the life cycle of Soleduck salmon and the challenges facing the fisheries industries. Just north of Forks, La Push Road connects Highway 101 with **Rialto Beach, Mora Campground** (part of Olympic National Park), and the Quileute native community of **La Push.** A short distance from the beach is ⊃**Manitou Lodge** (P.O. Box 600, Forks 98331; 800–841–0843 or 206–374–6295), which offers accommodations and an Indian craft shop that sells authentic Native American goods. Visitors to this secluded rain forest hideaway can take advantage of its proximity to forests, rivers, and beaches to enjoy a variety of outdoor activities and can relax by the huge lodge fireplace. Both breakfast and dinner are served in the lodge's friendly dining room. To get to Manitou Lodge, follow La Push Road eight miles west of Highway 101, turn right onto Mora Road, and then right again onto Kilmer Road after crossing the single lane bridge over the Sol Duc River. On the coast is **La Push Ocean Park Resort** (P.O. Box 67, La Push 98350; 800–487–1267), a Quileute tribal enterprise. Guests enjoy ocean views and access to miles of sandy and rocky beaches ideal for beachcombing. Whale-watching is a popular activity during the spring months.

Forks is primarily a logging town. The new **Forks Timber Museum** located south of town offers a comprehensive introduction to the history, economy, and culture of logging. Historical photographs, old logging equipment, and dioramas give a glimpse of what life was like in old logging camps and pioneer homes and how simple tools and hard work were employed to fell, transport, and cut timber into commercial lumber. The old-fashioned Fourth of July celebration in Forks highlights traditional logging skill competitions. For more information contact the Forks Chamber of Commerce, P.O. Box 1249, Forks 98331, or call (800) 44-FORKS.

For an intimate and fun way to explore the Olympic rain forests you can rent a bicycle at the **Olympic Mountains Bike Shop and Espresso Bar** (206–374–9777) on Highway 101 at the north end of town. A mountain bike is the ideal way to experience the rain forest's magnificent beauty. The area has hundreds of miles of low-traffic roads, logging roads, and single-track trails. Bike shop owner Lew McGill, who is also the local school superintendent, started the business to help diversify the Forks economy and to encourage his favorite sport. This is a full-service bike shop. You have a choice of high-quality bicycles to rent, directions for both on-road and off-road bicycling routes, and the town's best espresso and sweets for fuel. McGill will even organize a guided bicycle tour if visitors request.

The nicest place to stay in Forks is the ⊃**Miller Tree Inn** bed and breakfast (P.O. Box 953, Forks 98331; 206–374–6806), a 1917 homestead on three park-like acres located on East Division Street six blocks east of the only stoplight in town. Owners Ted and Prue Miller extend a hearty welcome to guests and can help organize a rewarding visit. The inn is especially popular with fishermen during the winter months, when breakfast from the big farmhouse kitchen is often served before dawn, and guests are sent on guided expeditions with a sack lunch and thermos of hot coffee. Combing ocean beaches, hiking over rain forest trails, and river kayaking are other popular activities. At day's end you can soak in the hot tub before a hearty dinner at one of several local restaurants.

Ten miles south of Forks is Upper Hoh Road, which follows the Hoh River Valley 18 miles east into the thickest part of the rain forest. At the end of the road is the Olympic National Park ⊃**Hoh River Visitor Center and Nature Trail.** This area receives over 120 inches of rain annually, creating a lush multi-layered environment highlighted with countless shades of green. Even a short excursion through the Hall of Mosses or along the Spruce Nature Trails offers an opportunity to experience the grandeur of the old-growth hemlock climax forest that once covered much of Western Washington. To reach more secluded parts of the forest, you can walk a few miles toward the Blue Glacier or take longer hikes to backcountry campsites such as Olympus (9 miles from the visitors center) or Glacier Meadows (an additional 8 miles). Write Olympic National Park Superintendent, 600 East Park Avenue, Port Angeles 98362, or call (206) 452–4501 for more information.

The **Rain Forest Hostel** (H.C. 80, Box 870, Forks 98331; 206–374–2270), located 23 miles south of Forks on Highway 101, offers basic accommodations at a minimal price. It's a popular base for young travelers exploring the Olympic Peninsula, so part of the fun is meeting visitors from around the world. Hosts Kay Ritchie and Jim Conomos go out of their way to help their guests explore the region, including arranging bike tours, rain forest hikes, fishing on the Hoh River, and visits to lumber mills and Indian reservations. A half mile south of the hostel is the turnoff west to the **Hoh Reservation Tribal Center.** The Hoh, like many native tribes, are working to maintain their heritage and continue their ceremonial and craft traditions. You are welcome to stop by the center to find out about the works of local weavers and other activities.

Highway 101 curves west to follow the cliffs above **Ruby** and **Kalaloch** (pronounced Clay-lock) beaches, offering magnificent views of the Pacific Ocean. It's a rugged and beautiful coastline where waves crash against rocks, driftwood, and offshore islands. This coast is littered with sea stacks, rock pillars that remain when coastal headlands are gnawed away by the powerful surf. The largest of these is Destruction Island, located 4 miles from shore. At night you'll see flashes from the island's lighthouse, which has provided a warning to coastal mariners since it was built in 1891.

At Queets the highway turns inland to Lake Quinault. This is the densest part of the rain forest. To experience this environment in maximum quiet and seclusion you can stay at ↄ**Lochaerie Resort** (638 North Shore Road, Amanda Park 98526; 206–288–2215), located four miles east of Highway 101 on the lake's north shore. The six rustic cottages have changed little since they were built on the cliffs above the lake in the 1920s and '30s. Named after Olympic Mountain peaks, each cottage has a fireplace, kitchen, and views of the lake—everything you need for a romantic sojourn. We are especially fond of cottage Ellinor, built in 1926, with its river-rock fireplace and large porch, where we spent our honeymoon. Lochaerie guests can explore the driftwood-covered beach, canoe, or hike nearby on rain forest trails.

On the south side of the lake, 2 miles east of the highway, sits **Lake Quinault Lodge** (P.O. Box 7, Quinault 98575; 800–562–6672 or 206–288–2571), a big, elegant waterfront resort built in 1926. The lodge sits above the lakeshore surrounded by beautifully maintained lawns and landscaping. Guests may rent boats and canoes for exploring the lake and enjoy badminton on the grass, games in the lobby, a swimming pool, and gourmet dining in the semiformal restaurant. In order to provide seclusion and rest, lodge rooms have neither telephone nor television.

Grays Harbor

The twin port cities of Hoquiam and Aberdeen on Grays Harbor are hard-working communities where logging, fishing, and shipping are everybody's business. On a hillside above residential Hoquiam you'll find the splendid ◗**Hoquiam Castle** (515 Chenault, Hoquiam 98550; 206–533–2005), built in 1897 by lumber baron Robert Lytle and now listed on the State and National Historic Register. For a small fee you can tour this restored mansion filled with opulent antiques, including beautiful cut-glass windows, a restored turn-of-the-century saloon, and a children's bedroom complete with hundred-year-old toys. You'll also enjoy a grand view of the cities from the castle's turret. Robert Lytle's brother Joseph, a partner in the lumber business, built a mansion next door in 1900. It is now the **Lytle House Bed and Breakfast** (509 Chenault, Hoquiam 98550). For a surprisingly reasonable rate you can stay in one of seven charming bedrooms, each furnished with antiques. Owners Robert and Dayna Bencala offer guests a warm welcome and an excellent breakfast in the morning. The mansion is also available for Murder Mystery Dinner Parties ("Whodunit? Somebody sitting at this table!") and other special events. Call the Bencalas at (206) 533–2320 for reservations.

Downtown Hoquiam has a waterfront park where you can watch work and pleasure boats on the river or climb the viewing tower at the end of Twenty-eighth Street on Grays Harbor to

Hoquiam Castle

watch ships being prepared for ocean journeys. You can continue west past Hoquiam to follow the coast north on scenic Highway 109, past a series of small resort towns including Ocean City, Copalis Beach, Pacific Beach, Moclips, and the native community of Taholah. Along the way are windswept beaches, art galleries, antiques and gift shops, and resorts. For more information on places to stay, contact the Washington Coast Chamber of Commerce at P.O. Box 562, Copalis Beach 98535 (800–286–4552 or 206–289–4552).

A few miles east of Hoquiam, the ꓷ**Aberdeen Museum of History,** located at 111 East Third Street in Aberdeen, includes an eclectic variety of curiosities and displays from Grays Harbor's past. You'll see yesteryear's logging and farming equipment, period clothing, and toys. Exhibits include a blacksmith's shop, a general store, and a one-room schoolhouse. There is even a model of Aberdeen's downtown before it burned in 1903. The museum is managed by an enthusiastic corps of volunteers who delight in sharing with visitors their personal memories of the area's history. It is open Wednesday through Sunday from 11:00 A.M. to 4:00 P.M. during the summer, and weekends from noon to 4:00 P.M. during the winter. Call (206) 533–1976 for more information, or contact the Grays Harbor Chamber of Commerce at 506 Duffy, Aberdeen 98520 (800–321–1924 or 206–532–1924).

Grays Harbor was a major shipbuilding center during the days of sail, when locally milled lumber was in great demand for hulls and spars. Three- and four-masted schooners, wooden steamships, and tugboats were constructed along the bay and crowded the harbor's docks. At the ꓷ**Grays Harbor Historical Seaport** (813 East Heron Street, Aberdeen 98520; 206–532–8611), you can absorb this sea history and tour a full-scale reproduction of the *Lady Washington,* one of the ships used by explorer Robert Gray to sail into the harbor in 1792. The replica was built in 1989 as part of the state's centennial celebration and now sails regularly along the coast. The seaport includes a large boat shop where visitors can watch boatwrights and volunteers build and maintain these beautiful vessels. There is also a chandler's shop, which sells an assortment of nautical gifts, and a visitors information center next door. To visit the seaport, follow signs that say "Tall Ships" to Aberdeen's harbor. Call ahead to find out about sailing and tour schedules.

Traveling south from Aberdeen you can either take Highway 101 directly south or meander west to the coast on Highway 105. A few miles down Highway 101 you'll pass the tiny logging community of **Artic,** a would-be Arctic misspelled by its founders. You won't want to miss a special treat at the rustic ⊃**Clark's Ice Cream Shoppe,** one of the few shops in Washington licensed to produce small batches of gourmet ice cream. The interior is a mixture of pioneer artifacts and tavern decor. The original owners, Ma and Pa Withrow, were a colorful pair who hand-fed the herds of elk that once frequented the area and wielded six-shooters to impress their customers. The logging camps and elk they once served have moved on, but their essence lingers.

To really get off the beaten path, turn east on North River Road just south of Artic and follow it 18 miles to **Brooklyn,** Washington. Although there is now little to mark the town except a school built in 1893 and a few houses, the road is gorgeous and has very little traffic. It's an ideal spot for a picnic. You can return to Highway 101 farther south on the equally beautiful Smith Creek Road.

Twenty miles west of Aberdeen just off Highway 105 you'll find the town of **Westport,** where maritime life is still very alive. The marina is always bustling as fishing and charter boats prepare for offshore tours or return loaded with fish and crabs. During the summer you can catch the passengers-only ferry from Westport across the mouth of Grays Harbor to Ocean Shores. The Westport boardwalk is an ideal place to watch the waterfront activity, and there's a tower to climb for a bird's-eye view. Westport's **Coast Guard Station** is now a maritime museum with complete skeletons of whales, a seal, and a sea lion.

March through May is the time to catch sight of migrating gray whales swimming north past Westport from their breeding lagoons in Baja California to the krill-rich waters of the Bering Sea near Alaska. For a moderate fee you can take a charter boat cruise to see these crusty but gentle leviathans. Once hunted to the brink of extinction, the gray whale population once again numbers in the thousands due to international protection. You'll be glad these amiable creatures are around when you watch their giant backs gracefully surface and dive before your eyes. To schedule a trip or find out more, call the Westport-Grayland Chamber of Commerce (800–345–6223 or 206–268–9422) for a breathtaking adventure at sea.

Willapa Bay

Following the coast south you'll have spectacular views of the open ocean before turning east at Willapa Bay. This long, shallow bay is rich with wildlife and shellfish. You can sample this bounty by following the turnoff at the Shoalwater Indian Reservation to the ↄ**Tokeland Hotel & Restaurant** (P.O. Box 223, Tokeland 98590), which boasts, "When The Tide Is Out The Table Is Set." The hotel's dining room offers a panoramic view of Willapa Bay as well as hearty food. Established in 1889 as the Kindred Inn, this is the oldest resort hotel in Washington state, offering simple but satisfying accommodations. The Grand Hall and Fireplace Room are ideal for socializing or relaxed reading. Call (206) 267–7006 for more information.

You can enjoy a public art treasure hunt by searching for the numerous historical murals that grace the walls of department stores, cafes, and public buildings in these coastal communities. A free Muralogue guide is available from the Long Beach Peninsula Visitors Center (P.O. Box 562, Long Beach 98631; 800–451–2542 or 206–642–2400). The guide gives directions to many of these artworks, although more are added every year. You'll find a variety of subjects, perspectives, and styles expressed in these delightful displays of community pride.

Raymond, located just south of the junction of highways 101 and 105, is a pleasant town on the Willapa River serving loggers, fishermen, and tourists. The old ↄ**Dennis Company** building at Blake and Fifth streets offers a glimpse of the region's history in a giant mural depicting shipping and logging activity in 1905. The 85-foot-long painting is one of the largest of Washington's historical murals. The Dennis Company store serves the lumber, farm, and fishing industries and also sells household goods. It's a friendly small-town general store with walls lined with tools and turn-of-the-century photographs. A collection of antique farm machinery and wagons across the street makes this a colorful corner to explore.

Continuing west on Highway 101, you'll pass through the picturesque riverside village of **South Bend.** The town's shoreline is worth a leisurely stroll to view the rough wooden fishing docks, piles of discarded oyster shells, and busy crab processing plants. The ↄ**Pacific County Historical Museum,** located on the highway at 1008 West Robert Bush Drive, offers glimpses of the area's colorful past. Walk up the hill behind downtown past some of the town's stately old houses for great views of the Willapa River and the forested hills that lie beyond. On the corner of Memorial and Cowlitz streets you can visit one of Washington's finest county courthouses. Open during business hours, the elegant 1910 building sports a beautiful art-glass dome and historical scenes painted in the 1940s by a prison inmate. For more information or to arrange a tour, call Pam Ekrem at (206) 875–5533.

The highway follows Willapa Bay's southeastern shore past South Bend. You'll pass rich wetland scenery including endless beds of eelgrass, feasting grounds for migrating black brant geese. The dynamic estuary environment supports a mind-boggling array of life-forms, from mud-dwelling clams, shrimps, and oysters to the millions of marine birds that consume them. After crossing the Naselle River, you'll pass pristine Long Island, part of ⊃**Willapa National Wildlife Refuge** and accessible only by private boat. The island supports a lush coastal rain forest that includes a stand of old-growth cedars as well as deer, bear, elk, grouse, beaver, and a diverse songbird population. Stop by the refuge headquarters east of the highway across from the island's south end for more information, or write to Refuge Manager, Willapa National Wildlife Refuge, Ilwaco 98624, or call (206) 484–3482.

Long Beach Peninsula

The Long Beach Peninsula is an inviting place to explore. The roar of the surf is never far off, the air is washed clean by ocean winds, and there are activities to suit any taste. The larger beach-side communities are popular tourist destinations, alive with a carnival atmosphere, but you don't have to go far to find lesser-known treasures and isolated spots for quiet contemplation.

Ilwaco is a hard-working fishing community at the peninsula's south end. The town's harbor is a great place to browse. You'll see charter boats seeking salmon, sturgeon, bottom fish, or tuna; canneries for fish and crab processing; fresh-fish markets; gift shops; and good food at friendly dockside eateries such as the **Reel Em In** diner. Ilwaco was the traditional point of entry for pioneers, vacationers, and supplies headed up the peninsula. Steamships and ferries from Oregon and California would unload supplies here and fill up with lumber and seafood for points south. The town was known first as Pacific City in the 1840s, then Unity when it was shifted west by military order in 1852, and finally Ilwaco, named after Chinook chief Elowahka Jim.

Between 1889 and 1930 the Ilwaco Railroad and Navigation Company transported goods and people up and down the peninsula, first by coach along the beach, then by narrow-gauge railway from Ilwaco to Nahcotta. A scale model of "the railroad that ran by the tide" is housed in a restored railway depot at the ↄ**Ilwaco Heritage Museum** (115 SE Lake Street; 206–642–3446). The museum is open year-round from 9:00 A.M. to 5:00 P.M. Monday through Saturday and noon to 4:00 P.M. Sunday. Children of all ages enjoy this charming display. The museum also features a fragrant collection of native plants, with information on their traditional tribal uses, and lots of local history. Ilwaco has five murals, including one across the street from the Heritage Museum honoring the Chinook tribe, "Grace of Land and Water." The first mural produced on the peninsula, a 1920s railway scene, can be found on the north side of the Doupe Brothers Hardware Store at the town's only traffic light.

The ↄ**Inn at Ilwaco** (120 Williams Street NE, Ilwaco 98624; 206–642–8686) is a fine bed and breakfast, located in an exquisitely refurbished church within walking distance of the port. The nine guest rooms, each with a private bath, were once Sundayschool rooms, the parlor was the high-ceilinged social hall, and the former sanctuary is now an auditorium used for performances, weddings, and receptions. Two and a half miles southwest of Ilwaco off Highway 101 is **Fort Canby State Park,** offering beaches, forest trails, campsites, and two historic lighthouses. From Memorial Day through Labor Day, weekend campsites at Fort Canby are available by reservation only. Call the Washington State Parks and Recreation Commission at (206) 753–2027 or the Fort Canby Park rangers at (206) 642–3078 for reservation information.

Waikiki Beach, a sheltered cove well supplied with driftwood and smooth sand near the park entrance, is a great place to watch the Columbia River's busy shipping activities. You can see giant freighters, laden barges pulled by colorful tugs, and fishing boats bouncing on ocean swells as breakers crash along the rocky

21

shore. For even more dramatic views, hike along the trails to the North Head Lighthouse, which looks west toward Hawaii and Japan. The ↄ**Cape Disappointment Interpretive Center** offers an exquisite vista of the Columbia between the north and south jetties. A stroll through the center takes you on Lewis and Clark's heroic journey from the Missouri to the Pacific. This exhibit has vivid descriptions of the expedition's activities as they struggled overland from the Midwest to the Pacific Northwest. You'll also find fascinating exhibits of historical maritime activities, with hair-raising descriptions of the lifesaving techniques once used to rescue sailors from sinking vessels along the rocky coast.

North on 101 is the town of Seaview, where you'll find several more murals. One depicting early public transportation adorns the Pacific Transit maintenance building just south of town. The mural shows Europeans traveling by horse-drawn carriage on the beach as they stop to speak with a Chinook family. Beaches along the peninsula continue to be used as a roadway and are classified as a Washington State Highway. You are allowed to drive a car on the upper beach area provided that you follow all state traffic laws but, since beach driving can damage both your car and the clam beds, we don't recommend it.

If you are in the mood for a leisurely stroll, Seaview's meandering back roads offer pleasant views of quaint cottages, many established during the late nineteenth century when this was a popular summer retreat. The ↄ**Shelburne Country Inn and Shoalwater Restaurant** (4415 Pacific Highway, Seaview 98644; Inn: 206–642–2442, Restaurant: 206–642–4142), hosted by David Campiche and Laurie Anderson, is the last active turn-of-the-century hotel on the peninsula. Built in 1886 and artistically restored in the 1970s, this elegant spot is known for its superb Pacific Northwest cuisine and warm hospitality. Along with antiques, homemade quilts, and a beautiful herb garden, the inn features hearty complimentary innkeeper's country breakfasts and gourmet meals.

Long Beach, the next town on your way up the peninsula, has a wooden boardwalk stretching 2,300 feet from South Tenth Street to Bolstad Street along the ocean beach, providing easy access to the heady interplay of roaring surf, rustling dune grass, and expansive vistas of smooth sand. Subtle lighting makes the boardwalk ideal for a romantic evening walk. The boardwalk is the place to view the endless array of multicolored kites that adorn the beach in late August during the **Washington State International Kite Festival.** To find out more about this special celebration, call the Peninsula Information Center at (206) 642–2400 or (800) 451–2542.

The ⊃**World Kite Museum and Hall of Fame** (P.O. Box 964, Long Beach 98631), tucked off the main road on Third Street in Long Beach, is the only kite museum in North America. The small, tastefully decorated museum features diverse displays, from delicate ancient butterfly and dragon kites to huge fighting kites and videos of kites in action on local beaches. Whether your interest is in their aerodynamic engineering, craftsmanship, or exquisite decoration, the kites in this museum are fascinating to see. The museum is open from 11:00 A.M. to 5:00 P.M. on weekends. Call (206) 642–4020 for more information. A few blocks south is a very different display: **Marsh's Free Museum,** which overflows with seaside kitsch. You'll want to bring along lots of quarters for the old arcade machines dotted throughout this store. Ponder the mystery of "Jake the Alligator Man" at home in the back of the store while you browse among shells, toys, antiques, and almost-junk.

Continuing north, the road remains divided from the sea by dunes, low shrubs, and grasses. Many condominiums and motels line the dunes, but you will find several entrances to the beach through public parks along the way, such as Loomis Lake and Pacific Pines state parks. You can walk to these ocean beaches on sandy paths lined with tiny wild strawberry plants. The beaches are great spots for seaside picnics and leisurely day hikes. **Klipsan Beach Cottages** has eight delightfully secluded cottages overlooking the ocean, each equipped with a full kitchen, cozy fireplace, and wooden deck 200 feet from the beach. We recommend visiting off-season, from October through May, Sunday through Thursday, for reduced rates and to better enjoy the solitude of this beautiful spot. For reservations, write to 22617 Pacific Highway, Ocean Park 98640, or call (206) 665–4888.

Head west (right) from Ocean Park on Bay Avenue and then north (left) on Sandridge Road to the tiny town of **Nahcotta.** Named for Chinook chief Nahcati in 1889, Nahcotta is the center of the peninsula's oyster industry. Native oysters, a tribal staple for centuries, were wiped out by the 1920s through overharvesting, disease, and freezing weather. The introduction of Japanese oysters (*Ostrea giga*) and new cultivation techniques, in concert with the favorable tidal action and relatively pristine water quality of Willapa Bay, has made this area one of the foremost oyster-growing spots in the world.

Nahcotta's ⊃**Ark Restaurant and Bakery** is famous for the regional culinary delights created by owners Nanci Main and Jimella Lucas. The modest blue building with its seaside gardens above docks and tidal flats offers superb meals featuring fresh local ingredients, including Willapa Bay oysters, Washington wild blackberries, Columbia River salmon, and sturgeon. The picturesque scenes through the Ark's large windows allow diners to reflect on the generous environment that produces such bounty. After such a wonderful meal you may be inspired to purchase one of the Ark cookbooks and try to recreate these masterpieces at home. The restaurant opens in summer for dinner at 5:00 P.M. and for Sunday brunch from 11:00 A.M. to 3:00 P.M. Hours are seasonal and the place fills up fast when open, so call (206) 665–4133 for reservations.

Just north of Nahcotta on Sandridge Road is Willapa Bay's earliest settlement, ⊃**Oysterville,** which is listed on the National Register of Historic Places. It's hard to believe that this quiet village was once a bustling commercial community. Established in 1854, Oysterville grew quickly as the center of oyster harvest activity, when shiploads of the bivalves were sent to delight the huge appetites of San Francisco. Oysterville was the county seat until 1893 when a posse of South Bend residents arrived by ship to fight for and win the right to move the county government. After native oyster beds were decimated in the 1880s, Oysterville became the quiet bayside village it remains today.

Beautiful **Oysterville Church** is a good place to start your visit. Stroll past Oysterville's well-maintained turn-of-the-century homes, one-room schoolhouse, placid woodlands, and friendly general store to absorb the rhythm of tides and weather that permeates this quiet little community. Three miles north of Oysterville on Stackpole Road is ⊃**Leadbetter Point State Park,** part of the Willapa National Wildlife Refuge. A favorite place for birdwatchers, the point's tidal flats overflow with migrating shorebirds and geese in April and May.

Along the Columbia River

The little town of **Chinook** was one of the most prosperous communities in Washington during the 1880s when fish traps lined the river, catching tons of fish to be processed in waterfront canneries. The traps were banned in 1935, and the once-busy community has settled into a restful retirement, but you can still see many lovely old homes built before the turn of the century. The old Methodist church on the corner of Highway 101 and Hazel Street has been converted into the elegant ⊃**Sanctuary Restaurant,** offering excellent food that highlights Scandinavian cuisine. You can try *fiskekaker* (fish cakes), *Svenska kottbullar* (meatballs), or the nightly seafood, meat, and produce specials. The Sanctuary is open for dinner daily except Mondays. It draws diners from all over the area, so we recommend that you call (206) 777–8380 for reservations.

Beautiful Highway 4 winds eastward through forest lands along the Columbia River, past the communities of Naselle, Grays River, Skamokawa, and Cathlamet. You may want to stop at the ⊃**Columbia White-tailed Deer National Wildlife Refuge,** with its 4,757 acres of diked floodplain and islands covered with thick grass and woodland habitat for birds and land animals. There are trails for walking or bicycling around the refuge.

The town of **Cathlamet** sits above the Columbia River, well situated for watching the parade of river traffic and enjoying views of the rural farmland of Puget Island. The 4-mile-long island is perfect for an easy bicycle ride (island roads are flat), and from the south end you can board the last of the Columbia River ferries. The ⊃**Wahkiakum County Historical Museum** at 65 River Street in Cathlamet offers artifacts of work and daily life from when the town was young. Visitors can stay at the **Cathlamet House** (225 South Second Street, Cathlamet 98612), built in 1895 by sea captain Ingram and renovated to its Victorian style by hosts Bill and Denice Hurd. Call (206) 795–3624 for reservation information. The 1907 **Country Keeper Bed and Breakfast Inn** (61 Main Street, Cathlamet 98612), was once the home of a local lumber baron. Guests now have a choice of four bedrooms from which they can watch the sun set over the mouth of the Columbia River. Call innkeepers Barbara and Tony West at (800) 551–1691 or (206) 795–3030 for more information.

Off the Beaten Path in the Puget Sound Region

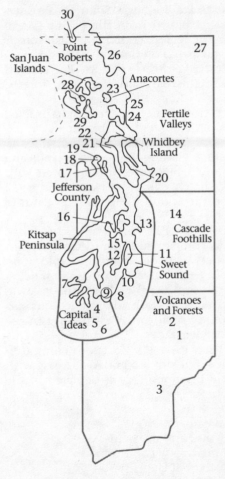

30

San Juan Islands

Point Roberts 26

27

28 23

Anacortes

25
24

Fertile Valleys

29
22
19 21
18
17
20

Whidbey Island

Jefferson County

16

14

13

Cascade Foothills

Kitsap Peninsula

15
12
11

Sweet Sound

7
10

9 8

Volcanoes and Forests

2

1

Capital Ideas 4
5 6

3

1. Mount Rainier Scenic Railroad
2. Pioneer Farm Museum
3. Mount St. Helens
4. Percival Landing
5. Wolf Haven Wildlife Sanctuary
6. Alice's Restaurant
7. Golden Grill Restaurant
8. Bair Drug and Hardware Store
9. Old Johnson Farm
10. Point Defiance Park
11. Sound Food Restaurant and Bakery
12. Puget Sound Mariners Museum
13. Center for Wooden Boats
14. The Herbfarm
15. Sidney Art Gallery
16. Suquamish Museum
17. Marrowstone Farm House
18. Rothschild House
19. Port Townsend Marine Science Center
20. Langley Cafe
21. Island County Historical Museum
22. Ebey's Landing National Historical Reserve
23. The Majestic
24. Skagit County Museum
25. Breazeale Interpretive Center
26. Tennant Lake Natural History Interpretive Center
27. Lynden Pioneer Museum
28. Little Portion General Store
29. Lopez Historical Museum
30. Point Roberts

Puget Sound Region

You could spend a lifetime exploring the Puget Sound region and still have more to discover. It's a landscape both grand and intimate. The lacy filigree of Puget Sound's inland waterways, cut by huge glaciers, has hundreds of miles of shoreline and numerous waterfront communities. Rivers washing sediment from the Cascade Mountains create the Puget Sound basin's fertile lowlands. Maritime weather blown from the Pacific Ocean carries abundant moisture to the region, supporting lush forests and farms. A dynamic economy based on natural resources, agriculture, and industry has attracted a diverse culture. The result is a unique interaction of mountains, farmlands, islands, forests, and people.

Until the mid-1800s, when white settlers arrived, Indians lived comfortably on the region's generous natural resources. Abundant salmon, cedar, herbs, and shellfish allowed the tribes to develop a sophisticated culture, including high-quality crafts and artwork. The people were proud, but peaceful compared with tribes farther north. Pockets of native culture still survive in small reservations scattered around the Sound, despite two centuries of disease, abuse, and neglect.

Puget Sound was named in 1792 for Lt. Peter Puget, the skilled and respected mariner who accompanied Captain George Vancouver on his world explorations. Vancouver left the exploration of the Sound's farther reaches to Lt. Puget, who commanded a flotilla of small boats to chart its intricate shorelines. The task was in good hands; in a few days Puget performed a meticulous survey that proved the impossibility of a Northwest Passage in the area and created charts of great accuracy.

The first generations of settlers created industrious communities in the forest-covered lands, but still celebrated the ease with which a simple lifestyle could be supported, as depicted in the last verse of the song "The Old Settler":

> No longer a slave of ambition
> I laugh at the world and its shams
> And I think of my happy condition
> Surrounded by acres of clams.

You can still find old-timers who'll tell stories of life, decades ago, when logging, fishing, and homesteading were the region's primary occupations; when the "mosquito fleet" of small steamships provided transportation between communities scattered along the Puget Sound shoreline; when the rhythm of the tides was a dominant force in every resident's life. Despite the changes that have occurred, people in the Puget Sound region still identify with this frontier tradition.

Many of the places described in this chapter preserve aspects of the region's historic, social, and environmental ambience. This is especially true of the Sound's numerous islands. Although it is increasingly common for residents to commute daily to the mainland for work, the island communities retain a strong sense of camaraderie, born in the days, not long ago, when the isolation of island life required both self-reliance and neighborly cooperation. There is not enough space in this book to cover all of these islands, but don't be afraid to stop on any of them for a day trip or weekend visit.

Several enjoyable and unique little communities described in this chapter give a big welcome to visitors. Steilacoom, Gig Harbor, Port Orchard, Poulsbo, Port Townsend, Coupeville, La Conner, and Lynden are popular favorites, each with special historic and artistic features. If these are too commercial for your taste during the summer season, you'll want to visit off-season. They are all friendly towns if you take time to get to know local folks.

The cities of Olympia, Tacoma, Seattle, and Everett form an urban corridor along the east side of Puget Sound. But even these urban areas offer exciting attractions that many visitors, and even residents, have yet to explore. You'll surely enjoy strolling along Olympia's colorful waterfront, visiting Tacoma's multiattraction Point Defiance Park, or renting a boat on Seattle's Lake Union.

Puget Sound is a haven for wildlife lovers. With a little luck you'll see seals frolicking along side your ferry boat, shorebirds dancing along deserted beaches, and raptors (birds of prey) soaring over the treetops. We recommend taking time to explore any of the area's wilderness parks and wildlife preserves, many of which include interpretive programs. But don't love these areas to death. Be careful to avoid disturbing wildlife or damaging the environment when visiting these public lands.

Volcanoes and Forests

Mount Rainier is a dominant feature of the lower Sound. There are many interesting places to visit in the area around Mount Rainier National Park. The steam-powered ⊃**Mount Rainier Scenic Railroad** excursion train takes riders on a slow jaunt from Elbe to Mineral Lake at the mountain's base. On this 1½-hour round trip you'll pass through thick evergreen forests, cross the bubbling Nisqually River, and enjoy spectacular views of the sleeping volcano's summit. Passengers can either sit in an open carriage or, if the weather is cool, relax in a closed car heated by a potbellied stove.

The musical duo Waltzing-in-the-Trees—Bill Compher on accordion and fiddle, Leslie Rousos on banjo and spoons—adds to the atmosphere with traditional songs, clogging, and railroad stories during the trip and the twenty-minute stop at Mineral Lake. Trains leave at 11:00 A.M, 1:15 P.M., and 3:30 P.M. weekends from Memorial Day through the end of September, and daily from June 15 through Labor Day. Special **Cascade Dinner Train Service** is provided Sunday afternoons (spring and fall) and Saturday evenings (during the summer). Elegant dinners are served by tuxedo-clad waiters in the renovated 1920s dining and observation lounge cars. This four-hour trip is an unforgettable experience. For information on train schedules and dinner reservations, call (206) 569–2588.

Back in the Elbe railroad yard, you'll find the two classic dining cars of the **Mount Rainier Dining Company** permanently parked on tracks—a 1922 Southern Pacific and a 1910 Great Northern, offering a railroad dining car experience for any meal. You can watch the steam engine switching in the yard while feasting on specialties such as salmon or baby-back ribs cooked over a fragrant wood-pit barbecue. Cooking takes place in a renovated 1910 baggage car. There is also a lounge named the Side Track Room (as in "Sorry, Honey, I got sidetracked") located in a late '30s Chicago-Burlington-Quincy coach. The dining car is open daily for breakfast, lunch, and dinner. Call (206) 569–2505 for reservations.

If all of this good food, drink, and adventure makes you drowsy, you can spend the night in one of the **Hobo Inn's** (206–569–2500) eight renovated cabooses, also located in the Elbe railroad yard. There are three 1916–1920 Southern Pacific

Mount Rainier Scenic Railroad

cabooses, three 1944 bay window cabooses used on the Milwaukee Road, and two 1954 cabooses used on the Chicago, Burlington and Quincy railroads. Each caboose has a modern bathroom, comfortable beds, and heating and air conditioning. From the cupola (the second-story tower on some cabooses) you'll enjoy a great view of railroad-yard activity and a chance to imagine life as a brakeman.

Six miles farther east on Highway 706 is Ashford, a small community of artists, outdoor enthusiasts, and old-timers who appreciate living at the entrance to Mount Rainier National Park. The **Mountain Meadows Inn** (28912 Highway 706, East Ashford 98304; 206–569–2788) is a friendly yet elegant bed and breakfast. Located in a house built in 1910, it was the home of the superintendent of National Mill, once the biggest lumber mill west of the Mississippi River and now a nearby ghost town. The house has been moved, renovated, and filled with an outstanding collection of railroad paraphernalia by host Chad Darrah, a retired logger and steam-train engineer as well as a jack-of-all-trades and local historian. Guests enjoy stories and music around the front-yard campfire stretching late into the night and wake to a hearty, homegrown, homemade country breakfast. Wildlife is often visible from the generous front porch or while strolling on trails through the forest. Unlike many bed-and-breakfasts, smoking is permitted here.

You'll find other unique treats in and around Ashford. **Growly Bear Bed and Breakfast** (P.O. Box 103, Ashford 98304; 206–569–2339), located on Goat Creek in a rustic 1890 homestead that once provided lodging for turn-of-the-century mountain visitors, offers guests delicious home-baked breads and pastries from their bakery to compliment their generous mountain breakfasts. There are plenty of art galleries in Ashford, and they all open their doors for Arttrek on the first Saturday of the month from 11:00 A.M. to 6:00 P.M. year-round, offering visitors an opportunity to discover the works of artists inspired by the grandeur of their mountain home. Highlights along the way include **Pottery by Jana,** whose charming studio on a quiet country road (30803 Mount Tahoma Canyon Road; 206–569–2933) offers functional stoneware enlivened with irises, and Doe Stahr's **Ravenware Gallery,** in town on Highway 706 (206–569–2865), which features black porcelain sculpture celebrating native Northwest Coast art.

If all this exploring has tied your muscles in knots, consider being pampered at **Wellspring,** where licensed massage therapist Sunny Thompson has created a mountain paradise of saunas, waterfalls, hot tubs, and gentle massage. Wellspring's studios are each self-contained; the outdoor hot tubs overlook landscaped gardens with terraced waterfalls and cooing doves. After a hike on Mount Rainier or a long bike ride to the mountain—or just to unwind—the wood-heat saunas or professional massage can do wonders to revitalize even the weariest traveler. Call (206) 569–2514 for more information.

In the lowlands near Eatonville you can enter a time warp at the ⊃**Pioneer Farm Museum** (7716 Ohop Valley Road, Eatonville 98328; 206–832–6300). The museum offers hands-on experience in pioneer living. Visitors forge horseshoes, grind wheat, or milk a cow long enough to have fun but not long enough to raise calluses. The museum's one-room schoolhouse is a reminder of the intimacy of education in rural communities. One-and-a-half-hour tours are run from 11:00 A.M. to 4:00 P.M. daily in summer and on weekends only during spring and fall. The museum gift shop, housed in an 1888 trading-post cabin, brims with old-fashioned treats.

North of Eatonville off Highway 161 is **Northwest Trek,** an unusual wildlife park where you can see a wide variety of wildlife, with emphasis on native North American species, living in a beautiful woodland setting. Endangered sandhill cranes and caribou roam free amidst moose, bison, and bighorn sheep, while elusive cougar, lynx, and bobcat prowl in Cat Country. You may catch sight of playful raccoons, river otters, or beavers as you explore the park's gentle nature trails adorned with ferns, native berries, and trees. The park opens at 9:30 A.M. daily from mid-February through October, with tram tours every hour beginning at 10:00 A.M. Closing times vary with the seasons. Write Northwest Trek Wildlife Park, 11610 Trek Drive East, Eatonville 98328, or call (206) 832–6116, for more information.

Your perspective of our world may change after you visit ⊃**Mount St. Helens,** "a mystic land of pumice, ash, and life (that) twists our traditional views, fascinates our imagination, and draws us closer to the heartbeat of the Earth." The living planet spoke on May 18, 1980, when St. Helens, one of the active volcanoes in the Pacific Ring of Fire chain, exploded in a massive outpouring of lava and dust. Since then, a total of 110,000 acres have been preserved for research, education, and recreation as the Mount St. Helens National Volcanic Monument. For back-door access to the mountain, take Highway 12 east from Interstate 5 to Randle, then turn south at the Adams and St. Helens Restaurant onto Forest Road 25. In six miles you can stop at the **Woods Creek Information Portal,** open daily from May through early October, for information about the volcano. Turn west toward the mountain on Forest Roads 26 or 99 for spectacular views and interesting interpretive presentations. The sudden bleakness of the terrain is tempered by Earth's tremendous regenerative power as new growth returns to the scarred land.

Highway 12 continues east through the Cascade Mountains and over White Pass, offering gorgeous views and numerous opportunities for outdoor exploration and sport. Packwood is the last community west of the pass. The nearby **Tatoosh Meadows** resort is a spectacular place to stay in the secluded meadows and evergreen forests adjacent to the headwaters of the Cowlitz River. Its cabins are ideal for a relaxed getaway at any time of the year, including winter when you can enjoy access to both downhill and cross-country skiing. There are no telephones or television, but there is plenty of entertainment just looking out the windows, fishing in the river, or walking on the forest paths. Although the land is rugged, guests enjoy maximum comfort in any of the seven cabins, which range from small studios to a full house. Owners Maree and Tom Lerchen include every detail: fully equipped kitchens, barbecue, private hot tubs, and wheelchair access. You can contact them by writing to Maree and Tom Lerchen, 27447 SE 401 Street, Enumclaw 98022 or by calling (206) 825–3693. Continuing east on Highway 12 takes you over the high mountain wilderness areas of White Pass, past the fishing resorts along Rimrock Lake, and down the lovely Tieton River Canyon toward Yakima.

Capital Ideas

Since **Olympia** is the state capital and the home of Olympia beer, many visitors simply tour the Capitol and the Olympia Brewery, then move on. But there are many lesser-known sights worth experiencing. You can start with a sidewalk tour of downtown as described in the Heritage Commission's "Olympia's

Historic Downtown: A Walking Tour," which highlights out-standing buildings, homes, and parks. This brochure is available from the Olympia Chamber of Commerce, located at 1000 Plum Street (206–357–3362) just off Interstate 5, next to the city's lovely Japanese Garden park.

Everybody loves to stroll along ⊃**Percival Landing** board-walk on Olympia's waterfront to see the arrival and departure of boats and ships and occasionally view the playful antics of a seal. A three-story tower at the Landing's north end offers great views of the port, the city, and on a clear day, the Olympic Mountains. You'll find several places to eat, including the **Olympia Farmer's Market,** located one block east on Thurston Avenue, where you can enjoy a delightful menu of just-harvested pro-duce, fresh seafood, and locally cooked specialty foods. The mar-ket is open from 10:00 A.M. to 3:00 P.M. weekends in April, Thursday through Sunday from May through September, and Fri-day through Sunday in October, becoming a Christmas market on weekends from November 1 through December 20.

To absorb the atmosphere of Olympia's past, enjoy a meal at the historic **Spar Cafe, Bar and Card Room** (114 Fourth Avenue East), which, as the name implies, offers patrons a choice of hearty food, drink, and entertainment. The Spar retains many details from its early days; chairs have a clip on the back to hold the patron's hat, sports scores are announced on a chalk board, and the walls are decorated with old logging photos (the name Spar refers to tall trees left standing to support the rigging used to load logs). The Spar still pumps its water from an artesian well located under downtown buildings. The restaurant opens daily at 6:00 A.M., closing at 9:00 P.M. Monday through Thursday, 10:00 P.M. Friday and Saturday, 3:00 P.M. on summer Sundays, and 8:00 P.M. on winter Sundays. The lounge and card room are open from 10:00 A.M. to 2:00 A.M. daily.

For delicious Northwest cuisine in an elegant atmosphere, dine at the **Seven Gables Restaurant** (1205 West Bay Drive NW), a beautiful Victorian mansion built in 1893 and renovated by cur-rent owner and restaurant manager Sally Parke. Located among terraced gardens on the bank above Budd Inlet, the Seven Gables provides spectacular views with your meal. The ambience is charming, the food is excellent, the staff is cheerful, and among the patrons you are likely to see the state's most influential politi-cians. The menu highlights local seafood, fine Washington wines, and farm-fresh produce for meals that melt in your mouth. If the weather is cooperative, you can reserve an outdoor table overlooking the bay. Seven Gables is open for dinner Tuesday through Saturday from 5:00 to 9:00 P.M. and for Sunday brunch from 9:30 A.M. to 1:30 P.M. Reservations are recommended because the Gables is very popular; call (206) 352–2349.

Directly across Budd Inlet, you can see the **Harbinger Inn Bed and Breakfast** (1136 East Bay Drive, Olympia 98506; 206–754–0389), located in the mansion built in 1910 by Victor E. Meyer. Innkeepers Marisa and Terrell Williams restored the house to its original beauty, including such details as stenciled wall paintings around the dining room and oak pocket doors. As well as warm hospitality and charming rooms, the inn features great views of the harbor and a serene backyard pond fed by an artesian waterfall. The inn is on some great bicycle routes as well as within walking distance of downtown and the lovely forest-to-bay trails of nearby **Priest Point Park.**

The **Puget View Guesthouse** (7924 Sixty-first Avenue NE, Olympia 98506; 206–459–1676), located a few miles northeast of Olympia on Puget Sound, has consistently ranked among the top Northwest bed and breakfasts because of its great service and spectacular waterfront location. From the guest cottage you'll enjoy views of Nisqually Reach, Anderson Island, and Longbranch Peninsula. Watch for marine wildlife, including seals, seabirds, and even killer whales, abundant in part because of the guesthouse's proximity to the **Nisqually National Wildlife Refuge.** The Nisqually River, which flows from glaciers on Mount Rainier, empties into Puget Sound at the refuge. This fertile river delta has been preserved for wildlife, providing a home to many animals and a major rest stop for migrating birds. Visitors can enjoy walking on the public trails, including the half-mile Nisqually River Loop, the one-mile Twin Barn Loop to the Twin Barn Education Center (open weekends from 10:00 A.M. to 2:00 P.M.), and the 5½-mile Brown Farm Dike Trail that loops around the refuge. Parts of the Dike Trail are closed during duck hunting season in autumn and winter. For more information, contact the refuge office at 100 Brown Farm Road NE, Lacey 98506; (206) 753–9467. The office is open from 7:30 A.M. to 4:00 P.M. weekdays. The refuge itself is open year-round during daylight hours. There is a $2 admission fee per family. Another recommended stop is the Nisqually Nature Center located on the shoreline at 4949

D'Milluhr Road NW, Olympia 98506 (206–459–0387). The center includes a collection of animal skeletons and other fascinating exhibits about the area's natural history. It is open from noon to 4:00 P.M. on Wednesdays and weekends.

A mystery awaits you a few miles south of Olympia at **Mima Mounds Natural Area Preserve,** an unanswered "whodunit" carved into the landscape. Just who or what made the mounded prairies that once covered much of Thurston and Lewis counties? Was it the fast motion of earthquakes on bogs, or the slow dirt accumulation on glaciers during the last ice age, or were they formed by ancient fish, by hordes of pocket gophers, or by native people creating burial sites—or are they perhaps the work of mythical Paul Bunyan? An interpretive center built into one of these six-foot-high geological bumps offers suggestions. You'll find an observation deck, a barrier-free interpretive path, and hiking trails among the riot of colorful wildflowers and native grasses that bloom in the spring. For a scenic route to the preserve, take Mud Bay Highway west from Olympia and turn south just past the Evergreen Parkway onto picturesque Delphi Valley Road. In about 5 miles veer right on Waddell Creek Road and follow signs south through the Capital Forest. In about 2 miles you'll see the turnoff to Mima Mounds on your right. For a more direct route, take Interstate 5 south from Olympia, go west from exit 95 on 128th Avenue past the town of Littlerock, turn right on Waddell Creek Road, and in about 1 mile you will see the Mima Mounds sign.

A few miles east of Mima Mounds is the **ↄWolf Haven Wildlife Sanctuary** at 3111 Offutt Lake Road, Tenino, open from 10:00 A.M. to 5:00 P.M. daily, May through September, and until 4:00 P.M. Wednesday through Sunday, October through April. Wolf Haven is a privately owned refuge for abandoned wolves and other feral animals that can't be returned to the wild. For a small fee you can take a tour. Volunteers describe wolf biology and lore as well as the personalities of individual wolves living at the sanctuary. Sanctuary staff often become so friendly with the animals that they will handle the wolves and even enter pens for some rough play. You can experience a howl-in on Friday and Saturday nights in summer (except in cases of heavy rain) from 7:00 to 10:00 P.M. Around a campfire you'll hear stories, roast marshmallows, sing along with folk musicians, and then howl in concert with the caged wolves. It's a wonderful, cathartic experience. You can also see peacocks, deer, and other wild animals wandering over the sanctuary grounds. To get to Wolf Haven, follow Capitol Way south from downtown Olympia as it becomes Old Highway 99, then turn left in 10 miles onto Offutt Lake Road, and in a little less than a quarter of a mile you'll see the entrance on the right. The phone number is (206) 264–HOWL.

South of Wolf Haven on Highway 99 is the town of **Tenino,** a friendly community, famous around the turn of the century for its sandstone quarries. In those days sandstone was a popular building material, and Tenino stone was both easy to cut and durable. To minimize freight costs the stone was carved to shape at each quarry by skilled stonecutters, many of whom were immigrants from Scotland. Eventually, the quarries closed as concrete replaced stone, but sturdy Tenino sandstone buildings can still be found all over the western United States. The beautiful **Tenino City Park** (located east of Tenino's main street off Olympia Street) was built around one of the retired quarries. Water cascades down moss- and vine-covered sandstone walls into a pond, now used each summer as the community's public swimming pool (open from 12:30 to 6:30 P.M., Tuesday through Sunday, from mid-June through August). Wooded nature trails lead upward to views of the pool and gardens.

Tenino was a railroad town named, some say, after the Number 10-9-0 engine that pulled local trains. Located on the main north-south line, all Olympia rail traffic used to change trains in Tenino. The **Tenino Depot Museum** adjacent to the city park is one of many local sandstone buildings. Museum exhibits illustrate techniques used in the old quarries to transform raw stone into everything from bricks to flower pots, as well as railroad lore and local history. Recently, interest in sandstone has revived and one of the quarries has reopened. Stonecarver Keith Phillips is often on hand at the museum to answer questions and share his enthusiasm for this ancient craft. Tenino also claims to be the home of the first legal wooden money, and the museum has the machine to prove it. The museum is open Thursday through Sunday, from noon to 4:00 P.M., from mid-March to mid-October. Call (206) 264–4321 for more information.

For outstanding dining in an out-of-the-way location, enjoy ⊃**Alice's Restaurant** (19248 Johnson Creek Road SE, Tenino; 206–264–2887). To get there, go south from Tenino on Highway

507, turn left at 184th Avenue (which becomes Skookumchuck Road), and in about 5 miles turn left onto Johnson Creek Road. Alice's Restaurant is located in a beautiful little valley next to award-winning **Johnson Creek Winery** (206–264–2100). The menu at Alice's highlights country game dinners—including braised rabbit, catfish, roast pheasant, and venison—in addition to more conventional fare. While waiting to be served, you can stroll around the trim gardens (complete with gazebo and back-yard ponds) or stop next door to sample premium Johnson Creek wines. You may want to take a few bottles of this limited-edition product home. Although Alice's is off the beaten path, it's a popular restaurant so be sure to make reservations.

Fifteen miles west of Olympia on Highway 101 is the lumber town of **Shelton,** dominated by the Simpson Lumber mill that sprawls along the waterfront. You can view the whole complex from the hilltop viewpoint adjacent to the huge sawmill wheel that stands as a monument to the lumber industry and a welcome to visitors who approach town from the east. A good place to start your exploration of Shelton is at the Chamber of Commerce Tourist Information Center located in an old caboose on Railroad Avenue in the center of town. Across the parking lot from the caboose, you can have a delicious meal at the ⊃**Golden Grill Restaurant** (324 Railroad Avenue; 206–426–2186), which features a large, circular Mongolian barbecue. Choose from an all-you-can-eat smorgasbord of ingredients to be fried, with great flair, in a few minutes while you watch.

Across the street, the **Mason County Historical Society Museum** offers exhibits of the region's logging and frontier past. Located in a library building constructed in 1914, the museum features family photographs, pioneer tools and artifacts, and a nineteenth-century schoolroom. The museum is open from noon to 5:00 P.M., Thursday through Sunday from June through September, and Thursday through Saturday from October through May. Stroll down Railroad Avenue and Cota Street to get a feel for the town. You'll discover that Shelton offers a wide selection of shops specializing in antiques and secondhand items. Some shops are meticulously arranged, others overflow in a happy jumble. Continuing north past Railroad Avenue, you will find a welcome green spot at Brewer Park. The park is flanked by brick buildings built over Shelton Creek, which runs through town parallel to Cedar Street. The Simpson Lumber headquarters across the street was designed to let this charming creek flow through a brick arch under its foundation.

Sweet Sound

Steilacoom is a small town perched on a bluff overlooking Puget Sound just south of the Tacoma Narrows. Established in 1854 by Maine sea captain Lafayette Balch, Steilacoom was the first incorporated town in the Washington Territories, and during the late nineteenth century was an important seaport, county seat, and commercial center. Visitors enjoy exquisite views of offshore islands and a stroll through the downtown National Historic District, with more than thirty buildings on the Historic Register. For all-out elegant dining, enjoy a sumptuous dinner at **E.R. Rogers Restaurant** (1702 Commercial Street; 206–582–0280), which serves only the best-of-the-best in food and drink. You can sample shrimp-stuffed artichoke, feast on charbroiled Northwest salmon, or try a combination platter of prime rib and Australian lobster tail. Dinners are served Monday through Sundays. The Sunday brunch offers an amazing all-you-can-eat buffet, including hot dishes, shellfish, seasonal fruits, and fresh breads and pastries. The restaurant occupies the restored mansion built by Steilacoom pioneer businessman Edwin R. Rogers in 1891 for his new bride, Catherine.

The old ⊃**Bair Drug and Hardware Store** (1617 Lafayette Street; 206–588–9668) offers lighter, less-expensive meals such as chowder, sandwiches, and homemade pie, or you can splurge with an ice cream soda from the original 1906 fountain. The store and pharmacy, built in 1895 by W. L. Bair, was popular with commuters who caught the Tacoma trolley that stopped across the street. Bair's had the first electric lights in Steilacoom; because they were on the same circuit as the trolley, the store's lights would dim just before the trolley arrived, giving patrons a few minutes warning to pay their bill. For decades the Bair Store was Steilacoom's favorite gathering spot, where residents swapped news around the potbellied stove. Bair's was restored in 1976 by the Steilacoom Historical Museum Association. Association volunteers collected traditional hardware and century-old patent medicines to fill the store's many display cases and installed the interior of the old Steilacoom Post Office. Rosa

Kreger now manages the store and restaurant under a lease with the Association. Bair Drug is open from 9:00 A.M to 6:00 P.M. during the summer and until 5:00 P.M. in the winter.

The name Steilacoom comes from the Indian name for fringe-cup, a small flower abundant in the area. The indigenous people of south Puget Sound, the Coast Salish, had a main village where the town of Steilacoom is now situated. Although the tribe was well established at the time, it was not officially recognized by the United States government in the Medicine Creek Treaty of 1854 in order to avoid committing any of the valuable land along the Sound to Indian reservations. Despite being officially ignored, the Steilacoom tribe has preserved its identity and traditions. You can learn more by visiting the **Steilacoom Tribal Cultural Center,** in a beautiful old church in downtown Steilacoom (1515 Lafayette Street; 206–584–6308). The center is open daily except Monday from 10:00 A.M. to 4:00 P.M. The center includes three galleries: Gallery I displays exhibits on Native American themes, which change every two to six months; Gallery II features the history and contemporary life of the Steilacoom tribe; Gallery III maintains the permanent exhibit "Visions of the Past: Legacy of the Steilacoom Tribe," which was created for the Washington State Centennial celebration. The gift shop sells Indian crafts and artwork. There is a small admission charge for some exhibits.

Steilacoom's history is rich with stories of fast ships, quick business deals, and slow trains. To learn more about the town, visit the **Steilacoom Historical Museum,** in the basement of the Town Hall at 112 Main Street (206–584–4133). The museum, open from 1:00 to 4:00 P.M. Tuesday through Sunday, offers a glimpse of the town's 140-year history, including displays of a turn-of-the-century kitchen, a blacksmith's shop, and a barber shop.

From Steilacoom you can take a pleasant half-hour ferry ride to Anderson Island. The island is only 4 miles from end to end, but there are plenty of little nooks to explore. The island community takes pride in its pioneer history. At the center of the island you'll find the ⊃**Old Johnson Farm,** which was farmed by the Johnson family from 1912 to 1975 and is now maintained by the Anderson Island Historical Society to display the labors and comforts of traditional rural life. A community garden on the property brims with homegrown vegetables and fruit in summer and fall. Tools and artifacts are on display, including the wheelhouse of the ferry *Tahoma*, which plied the Anderson Island route for decades. The farm is always open and tours of the farmhouse are available on summer weekends. Call (206) 884–2135 for more information.

Anderson Marine Park, on the island's southwest shore, is a delightful secluded place to explore. The park has an enjoyable nature trail through the woods and down to Carlson's Cove. Well-marked signs point out the diverse plant life and bird activity in the lush evergreen forest through which you walk. Along the way you'll step on short stretches of the trail marked "skid road," "corduroy," and "puncheon." These terms, which describe the shape of the logs under your feet in the muddier parts of the walk, demonstrate historic road surfacing techniques to show how logging roads were once built. Each step of this well-tended path is a testament to island pride. The last stretch includes a steep descent down to a small dock floating in the secluded cove rich with intertidal life. Beware of the poison oak beyond the marked path along the shore and be sure to wear good walking shoes.

Ken and Annie Burg offer families the fun and comfort of their renovated log homestead, the **Inn at Burg's Landing,** located just down the beach from the Anderson Island ferry dock. From the inn's large picture window, visitors can watch the ship and boat traffic passing on Puget Sound, with a backdrop of Mount Rainier and the Cascades. Depending on the season, you may want to while away your time in the outdoor gazebo, complete with hot tub, or seek comfort in the large wood-heated living room. The inn's private beach is ideal for a stroll and seashell collecting. Ken Burg, who grew up on Anderson Island and attended its one-room school, can tell stories of island life "back in the good old days" when it was a quiet and isolated community. Annie guarantees that no guest goes hungry for breakfast. For reservation information, call the Burgs at (206) 488–8682 or 884–9185, or write to them at 8808 Villa Beach Road, Anderson Island 98303.

The city of Tacoma has received a bum rap, in part because of the strong smell from the city's paper mills and other industries. But visitors who take the time to explore the city are amply rewarded. Many of Tacoma's older commercial and residential buildings are being renovated (some would say "gentrified"), creating delightful neighborhoods. **Old Town** is one of these renovated areas, located a mile northwest of downtown at North Thirtieth Street and Ruston Way. The nearby Commencement Park is the eastern end of a 2-mile scenic waterfront promenade that offers bicyclists and walkers wonderful views, restaurants, parks, a historic fireboat, and plenty of beach access. Ruston, a small community that is now a suburb of Tacoma, has a pleasant commercial district that includes the **Antique Sandwich Shop** at 5102 Pearl Street, a popular hangout. Local musicians perform there on weekend evenings, and in good weather you can enjoy your meal outside in the Garden of Eatin'. Also along Pearl Street are a number of antique shops.

Pearl Street ends to the north at ⊃**Point Defiance Park.** This outstanding 698-acre park offers plenty for everybody. You can visit the zoo and aquarium (which has a fascinating shark exhibit); tour the historic **Fort Nisqually,** which includes some of the oldest buildings in Washington state; ride a train and learn about the days of steam logging at **Camp 6 Logging Museum;** explore several spectacular gardens; or rent a small boat complete with fishing gear for relaxation on the Sound. The **Boathouse Restaurant** offers good meals and great views of Commencement Bay. There is even a ten-acre **Never Never Land** where, for a small fee, you can stroll among famous characters from children's literature, a treat for young kids. Scenic **Five Mile Drive** circles the park, offering multiple perspectives of Puget Sound waterways. For more information, contact the Metropolitan Park District of Tacoma at 5400 North Pearl Street, Tacoma 98407; (206) 591–3690.

Point Defiance is also where the ferry leaves for **Vashon Island,** one of the largest of Puget Sound's islands. Call (800) 542–0810 for ferry schedule information. Despite its proximity to both Seattle and Tacoma, Vashon retains its charming rural character. It's also a hospitable community to visitors. At Vashon Center, you'll find hearty and healthful food at ⊃**Sound Food Restaurant and Bakery,** open daily at the corner of Vashon Highway and Ellisport Road (206–463–3565), a favorite stop for the many bicyclists who tour Vashon. Nearby in a Victorian-style building you'll find the **Country Store and Farm** (20211 Vashon Highway Southwest), where you can buy farm-fresh products, practical clothing, and gifts seven days a week. Sample the fruits of Vashon's thriving visual and performing arts community at the **Blue Heron Art Center,** open Tuesday through

Never Never Land

Saturday from 12:00 to 5:00 P.M. Located in a 1912 historic landmark at 19704 Vashon Island Highway SW (206–463–5131), the center features exciting monthly exhibits, concerts, dances, and workshops. Numerous other art galleries and specialty shops, and bed and breakfast guest houses, are scattered over the island. Write the Vashon Business Association at P.O. Box 1035, Vashon 98070, or call (206) 463–2257 for a list.

Gig Harbor is a delightful maritime community nestled in a protected bay on the northwest side of the Tacoma Narrows. It was first explored by Europeans in 1841 when members of Charles Wilkes expedition navigated the sheltered bay in gigs, small boats that gave the town its name. The harbor is now crowded with pleasure and fishing boats. Visitors in town mingle with the hard-working fishing families and artists who inhabited Gig Harbor before it became a popular tourist spot. Harborview Drive, which hugs the shore, is lined with shops, sidewalk cafes, and galleries, making it a great place to stroll. If the weather is warm, you'll want to treat yourself to **AJ and Charlie's** special handmade ice cream, at 3026 Harborview Drive.

For a fun and inexpensive overview of the harbor, you can ride the bright red, open-air trolley bus that circles through town on weekends from mid-June through early September. Trolleys run from 11:00 A.M. to 7:00 P.M. on Saturdays and until 5:00 P.M. on Sundays. A donation of fifty cents is requested. Call (206) 383–1085 for more information. The trolley winds up the hill to **Celebrations Meadow,** at 9916 Peacock Hill Avenue Northwest, where you can experience the sensation of losing and finding yourself amid the pathways of a fir-scented maze. Both adults and children have a great time navigating in and out of this giant puzzle. The maze is open from 10:00 A.M. until dusk, April through October, and on weekends in the winter. The surrounding meadows form a natural amphitheater where musical performances enliven weekend evenings throughout the summer. The Gig Harbor Jazz Festival gets the meadow swinging in August. Next door, **Celebrations Restaurant** (206–851–7930) offers fine dining from its hilltop setting. Located in a big Victorian-style home, the restaurant is open Wednesday through Friday from 11:00 A.M. to 9:00 P.M., Saturdays from 5:00 to 9:00 P.M., and on Sundays for brunch from 10:00 A.M. to 2:00 P.M. and for dinner from 4:00 to 9:00 P.M.

Gig Harbor's **Rent-A-Boat and Charters** (8827 North Harborview Drive; 206–858–7341) offers several fun ways to explore Puget Sound, from pedal boats and seagoing kayaks to large sailboats and powerboats. Located below Neville's Restaurant, the operation is open daily (weather permitting) in spring and summer from 9:00 A.M. to 7:00 P.M. and by reservation in winter. You can also see Puget Sound through the eyes of Gig Harbor's many talented artists. Galleries. featuring local artisans are scattered throughout the town, with a special Gallery Walk held the first Saturday of every month from 10:00 A.M. to 8:00 P.M. Highlights include the **Ebb Tide Co-operative Gallery** (8815 North Harborview Drive; 206–851–5293), open daily until 5:00 P.M., which shows handmade delights, from colorful woven clothing to wood carvings and pottery. **St. Hill Art Gallery,** open daily from 10:00 A.M. to 6:00 P.M., is next door at 8825 North Harborview Drive and features local paintings and raku as well as quality art supplies.

You can explore Gig Harbor's maritime history at the ⊃**Puget Sound Mariners Museum,** a treasure chest of model ships, photographs, and navigational tools, at the southwest end of Harborview Drive. The museum is run by friendly volunteers Wednesday through Sunday from noon to 4:00 P.M., or you can arrange a special tour by calling (206) 858–SALT.

Seattle's International District, south of downtown and east of the Kingdome, includes a large and well-established Asian community. Visitors enjoy touring the many small shops and sampling the excellent food. **Uwajimaya,** at 519 Sixth Avenue South, is a unique department store where you'll find an amazing assortment of Asian foods and household goods. The aisles, crowded with a mind-boggling array of intriguing items, give the uninitiated a taste of life in a different culture. Upstairs you'll find exquisite artworks, furniture, and books from across the Pacific. To learn about Seattle's Chinese community, contact **Chinatown Discovery, Inc.,** which offers both day and night guided tours of the Chinese/Asian Museum, specialty shops, and the district's best restaurants. Chinatown Discovery is owned and operated by Vi Mar, an active member of the Chinese American community who works to ensure that your tour is both entertaining and meaningful. Contact Chinatown Discovery at (206) 236–0657.

Lake Union in the heart of Seattle is about as on-the-beaten-path as you can get, yet many people don't know that the

⊃**Center for Wooden Boats,** at the south end at 1010 Valley Street, has a fleet of classic wooden boats, lovingly built and maintained, which are available for rent by the hour or the day. You can choose a simple rowing dory, a kayak, or a lapstrake sailing skiff to explore Seattle's waterway attractions and join the colorful flotilla of small boats on Lake Union. The center also sponsors workshops where enthusiasts share ancient skills and historical knowledge, from boatbuilding and knot work to traditional music and lore of the seven seas. The center's pavilion is an ideal place to enjoy a picnic and view lakeside activities. There is always something interesting going on. For more information call the center at (206) 382–BOAT.

Adjacent to the Center for Wooden Boats are the three towering masts of the historic wooden schooner *Wawona,* the last survivor of the fleet of commercial sailing ships that once plied the waters of the Pacific Northwest. The 165-foot *Wawona* was built in 1897 and worked for half a century carrying lumber along the Pacific coast and fishing in the Bering Sea. Now being renovated by the Northwest Seaport organization, her classic beauty is emerging after decades of neglect. Visitors can walk on the deck, where sailors once handled the immense sails, tour the officers' cabin at the stern and the crew's crowded quarters in the fo'c'sle (pronounced "folk-sull" from "fore castle"), and go below into the cargo hold.

Cascade Foothills

The picturesque **Snoqualmie Valley,** a few miles east of Seattle, is surrounded by the foothills of the Cascade Mountain Range. The valley is filled with small farms, friendly communities, and evergreen forests. The Snoqualmie River, flowing down the valley, creates the spectacular 268-foot Snoqualmie Falls. Above the falls is a public overlook and the beautiful but relatively expensive **Salish Lodge** (37807 SE Snoqualmie Falls Road, Snoqualmie 98065) hotel and restaurant. Call (800) 826–6124 or (206) 888–2556 for reservation information. The **Old Honey Farm Country Inn** (8910 384th Avenue SE, Snoqualmie 98065; 800–826–9077 or 206–888–9399) offers comfortable bed and breakfast accommodations at a more reasonable price.

The falls and town of **Snoqualmie** have attracted tourists seeking outdoor adventure for over a century. Hundreds once arrived each weekend on excursion trains from Seattle. The **Puget Sound & Snoqualmie Valley Railroad** once again offers train rides from the beautifully restored Victorian train station in downtown Snoqualmie, through scenic evergreen forests, to the nearby community of North Bend and past Snoqualmie Falls. There are runs each weekend from April through October (Sundays-only before Memorial Day and after Labor Day). Call (206) 746–4025 for schedule and fare information.

A few miles below, near Fall City at the confluence of the Raging and Snoqualmie rivers, is ↄ**The Herbfarm,** at 32804 Issaquah-Fall City Road, a nursery, specialty shop, and restaurant where you can see, smell, and taste over 600 different herbs and plants. You'll find delightful tools and concoctions for your garden, kitchen, and bath. Guests are welcome to tour the farm's 17 gardens and enjoy special events from seasonal celebrations to gardening and cooking classes. Meals at the award-winning and very exclusive Herbfarm Restaurant begin with a hosted garden tour, then move indoors for a three-hour, six-course lunch or thematic nine-course dinner. The innovative menus change with the season to take advantage of the freshest produce and seafood. Many of the ingredients are harvested from the garden minutes before being cooked. Lunch is served most Fridays, Saturdays, and Sundays; dinners are served only on special occasions. Reservations are required, sometimes months in advance, due to limited seating capacity. Call (206) 784–2222 for information. To reach the Herbfarm from Highway 202 in Fall City, turn south on 332nd Avenue SE, then follow it right onto 46th Street/Issaquah-Fall City Road.

You'll find more farms to explore near **Carnation,** 6 miles north of Fall City on Highway 203. **Remlinger Farms** is a diverse 270-acre fruit, vegetable, and berry farm that welcomes families for a visit to the country. There's a free farm-animal petting zoo for children, picnic tables, a farm-fresh produce store, restaurant, and bakery. The farm has seasonal festivals at various times of the year. Many customers go into the fields to pick their own berries and vegetables. Farmer Gary Remlinger promises "true farm atmosphere" and "the very freshest produce at the lowest direct-farm prices." Remlinger Farms offers a Ripe 'n Ready Report of in-season produce by calling (206) 451–8740 or

333–4135. The farm is located half a mile off Highway 203 on Northeast Thirty-second Street, just south of Carnation.

The nearby **Carnation Farm,** "home of contented cows," was established as a research facility in 1910 by E. A. Stuart, founder of the Carnation Company, in order to help increase Washington state's milk production for use in his condensing process. The Carnation Farm is an idyllic 900-acre facility that includes the first statue erected to a cow (Segis Pietertje Prospect, who set a world record in 1920 by producing 37,381 pounds of milk in one year), experimental flower gardens, a modern milking facility, and a retirement home for Friskies pet-food canine and feline professional tasters. The farm is open for tours Monday through Saturday from 10:00 A.M. to 3:00 P.M., March 1 through October 31. To reach Carnation Farm, go 1 mile north of Carnation and turn west onto Northeast Sixtieth Street/Carnation Farm Road. For information call (206) 788–1511.

Kitsap Peninsula

Port Orchard has a hospitable downtown that is ideal for window shopping. Bay Street, the main commercial street, has old-fashioned sidewalks with a wooden canopy for comfortable strolling, rain or shine. Murals on downtown walls illustrate life during the late nineteenth century when Port Orchard was a major stop for the mosquito fleet, the small steamboats that were once a common form of transportation on the Sound. On the north end of Sidney Avenue you can catch the modern version of the fleet, which carries pedestrians and bicycles across the bay to Bremerton every half hour. A waterfront observation deck offers views of marine activities in the bay and across the water in Bremerton's naval shipyards.

You'll get a taste of Port Orchard's early days as well as the richness of local artistic talent by strolling a few blocks south up Sidney Avenue to the ⊃**Sidney Art Gallery.** The gallery at 202 Sidney Avenue (206–876–3693) is open Tuesday through Saturday from 11:00 A.M. to 4:00 P.M. and on Sunday from 1:00 to 5:00 P.M. The first floor of this former Masonic Temple, built in 1903, features monthly exhibits highlighting the works of talented Northwest artists. On the second story is a museum with exhibits of turn-of-the-century stores and coastal scenes. For a special meal while in Port Orchard, enjoy the Nakkour family's gracious hospitality and authentic Lebanese cuisine at **Hadi's Restaurant** (818 Bay Street; 206–895–0347), which transports you to the ancient Mideast. Try the house special, which includes a sample of various delicately spiced foods, from stuffed grape and cabbage leaves to charbroiled chicken and lamb. The hoummos (chick-pea and sesame pâté) is delightful, as is the honey-sweetened baclava served for desert with mint tea or rich Arabic coffee. Hadi's is open from 11:00 A.M. to 9:00 P.M. Monday through Saturday.

Down the street, on the corner of Sidney and Bay, Fred and Ruth Karakas have a great way to work off your meal. Their **Olympic Schwinn** bike shop rents everything a family needs (including bicycle trailers and helmets) to enjoy a splendid ride on the Manchester Bike Route. This is a quiet, winding, beach-front road that goes 15 miles to Manchester. Along the way you'll find beaches to explore, a restaurant where you can refuel, and a pleasant state park for play. For an all-day adventure, you can bicycle approximately 8 miles further to the Southworth Ferry Dock and ride a ferry to Vashon Island or downtown Seattle. Olympic Schwinn is open Monday through Friday from 10:00 A.M. to 7:00 P.M. and Saturdays until 6:00 P.M. Call (206) 895–4248 for information.

When tired and hungry cyclists seek the area's best hospitality, Fred and Ruth Karakas have two recommendations. **Ogles Bed and Breakfast** (1307 Dogwood Hill SW, Port Orchard 98366; 206–876–9170) is a pleasant home on a bluff overlooking the bay, just off Bay Street on the west edge of town. Quentin and Louise Ogle offer substantial servings of hospitality and breakfast to their guests at a reasonable price. **Reflections Bed and Breakfast** (3878 Reflection Lane East, Port Orchard 98366; 206–871–5582), a spacious home filled with New England antiques, offers magnificent views of Bainbridge Island and Port Orchard Passage from each guest room, the deck, or the hot tub. Guests can choose from the Chesapeake Room (with a handmade sunflower quilt on an old-fashioned twin-poster bed), the Sudbury Room (with an antique spindle bed), the Fairfax Room (blue-and-white trim with an antique iron-and-brass bed), and the honeymoon suite complete with a private sitting room and deck.

Poulsbo is a friendly community on the shores of Liberty Bay. Settled in the 1880s by Norwegians and dominated by this cultural and language group until World War II, the Poulsbo business community has revived this heritage to create a Scandinavian theme town. Scandinavian delights await you at every turn in the town's historic district, from potato *lefse* (pancakes) to the painted folk art designs (*rosemailing*) adorning shutters and doorways downtown. Like other popular tourist destinations, Poulsbo can be crowded on summer weekends so you may prefer to visit a little off-season.

Shops featuring delicious treats abound on Poulsbo's historic Front Street: the sweet-smelling **Sluy's Poulsbo Bakery** offers traditional Scandinavian baked goods, **Poulsbo Drugstore and Fountain** features an old-fashioned soda fountain and giant cones, **Boehm's Chocolates** will satisfy the sweetest tooth, **Ye Olde Copper Kettle** serves English tea with scones and cucumber sandwiches, and **New Day Seafood Eatery** (325 NE Hostmark, 206–697–3183) serves up fish and chips and other fresh seafood dishes and offers patrons views of the town and Liberty Bay. Other delights include the **Cargo Hold,** which overflows with nautical gifts, and **Leslie's Place** (19003 Front Street; 206–779–2111), a contemporary art gallery and espresso bar on a bluff overlooking the bay, which sponsors Saturday evening poetry and fiction readings and music performances. Leslie's is open Monday through Saturday from 10:00 A.M. to 7:00 P.M. (until 9:00 P.M. on Tuesdays), and on Sundays from noon to 4:00 P.M.

The **Marine Science Center,** at 17771 Fjord Drive NE, celebrates Poulsbo's proximity to the sea. Established in 1966, the center offers a hands-on introduction to coastal marine life. Children are fascinated by the touch tanks filled with living sea creatures such as kelp crabs, sea cucumbers, and anemones. Teaching exhibits present important concepts of marine biology and history in clear and aesthetically pleasing displays. For more information and hours, call (206) 779–5549 on weekdays.

One of the best features of Poulsbo is its parks. When you've tired of browsing in the shops or learning about marine biology, head for **Anderson Parkway** with its large wooden gazebo (Kvelstad Pavilion), where you can relax before the view of boats, Liberty Bay, and the green hills beyond. A 612-foot boardwalk leads from the Viking statue, along the shore, and up the forest-covered bluff to the serene **Arboretum Conservatory.** As you stroll you may see an elegant loon or cormorant dive for fish just offshore.

A right (south) turn off Highway 305 south of Poulsbo takes you to the つ**Suquamish Museum,** which will introduce you to the history and traditional lifestyle of the Suquamish Nation. Exhibits juxtapose ancient and modern ways. Ironwood digging sticks, traditional canoes, and diagrams of spearfishing are shown alongside photos of the tribe's current fish propagation program. A walk-through longhouse supported by carved wooden house-posts leads to an auditorium where visitors can watch "Waterborne: Gift of the Indian Canoe." This thirteen-minute slide/tape show illustrates the Suquamish tribe's canoe building and salmon restoration projects, powerful images celebrating the renewal of a rich cultural heritage. The museum is open daily from 10:00 A.M. to 5:00 P.M. in summer, and Friday through Sunday from 11:00 A.M. to 4:00 P.M. in winter. Call (206) 598–3311, extension 422, for more information.

Three miles northeast of the museum off Highway 305 is **Old Man House State Park,** where Chief Sealth (who gave his name to the city of Seattle) lived and died. The Old Man House was a huge plank building that once stretched along the beach. A display explains how local tribes built and used the gigantic house. The park is beautiful, although tiny, ideal for picnics and quiet reflection alongside Agate Passage.

For a relaxing rural interlude, we recommend the **Manor Farm Inn** (26069 Big Valley Road NE, Poulsbo 98370; 206–779–4628), an elegant bed and breakfast for people in need of refuge from hectic modern life. From the farm's courtyard you can look over green fields lined with rustling poplar windbreaks, hear barnyard animals, and contemplate twined roses climbing the trellises. Rooms feature simple but beautiful French pine antiques, original watercolors, down comforters, and fresh flowers. Guests are pampered with fresh-baked scones and coffee delivered to their bedroom door each morning. After a hearty country breakfast, you can relax under fruit trees or stroll past well-tended sheep, pigs, and chickens to a trout pond out back where guests try their hand at fly-fishing. Bikes are available to ride through the pleasant countryside and for exploring the nearby towns of Poulsbo and Port Gamble. The inn also features an outdoor hot tub and a drawing room for board games and other quiet entertainment. Four-course dinners are served in the elegant dining room, a different gourmet delight each night. The inn caters to adults, so children must be at least 16 years old.

Port Gamble (2 miles east of the Hood Canal Floating Bridge, on Highway 104) is home of the Pope and Talbot Mill, the oldest continuously operating sawmill in North America. The immaculate town, modeled after its founders' home in East Machias, Maine, is a bit of nineteenth-century New England transplanted to the West Coast. It is a true company town; the charming old homes that you see are owned by the mill and inhabited by its employees. You can pick up a Historical Walking Tour brochure that describes many of the town's homes and their history at the eclectic **Port Gamble Country Store** (206–297–2623). The center of town activity since its inception in 1853, the store has everything from milk to gourmet jams and rain boots. Upstairs you'll find a huge collection of shells in the **Sea and Shore Museum** (hours vary according to the season; call 206–297–2626 for more information). Down the hill, the **Port Gamble Historical Museum** provides further insight into the town's colorful history (open daily in summer, or call 206–297–3341 to arrange visits during other seasons).

Jefferson County

The **Weatherford** bed and breakfast is located just south of the Hood Canal Bridge, on Shine Road. This charming cedar-shingled inn with big picture windows sits on a grassy hillside dotted with wildflowers above Suquamish Harbor. The three guest rooms offer spectacular views of Puget Sound and beautiful fields of wildflowers. One suite is wheelchair-accessible and all are tastefully decorated with fine furniture, fresh flowers, and quality linen. The Sherlock Holmes room features Sir Arthur Conan Doyle's books as well as a gift hidden in a secret drawer for sleuths-in-the-making. Gourmet breakfasts are included, and other meals, including picnics on the beach, are available with advance requests. Contact the innkeeper at 941 Shine Road, Port Ludlow 98365, or call (206) 437–0332.

Shine Road becomes Paradise Bay Road north of Highway 104, which winds through the forests above Hood Canal, offering occasional glimpses of the water along the way. Past Port Ludlow and Oak Bay you can turn off to Indian Island and Fort Flagler or you can continue straight toward Port Townsend. The bridge to **Indian Island** offers great views of the narrow strait separating this island from the mainland. The road beyond the bridge follows the southern shore, with several places to pull off and admire the scenery. Turn right at the Jefferson County Day Use sign and follow the gravel road down to the beach to explore the pebbly tidelands, scattered with driftwood and salt marsh plants. Myriad water birds are especially abundant during their fall migration. Just above the shore you'll find the trailhead to the South Indian Island Trail, an ideal hike if you want to explore more of the island's beauty.

The causeway from Indian Island to **Marrowstone Island** crosses lush wetlands and a lagoon between the two islands. Nearby sits **The Ecologic Place,** a rustic, peaceful retreat surrounded by tall grass and wild beaches, ideal for wildlife lovers. Cedar guest cabins encircling the meadow beyond the house are clean but not fancy. Their windows offer enchanting views of Oak Bay. The sound of fledgling swallows, the sight of aquatic birds bobbing on the bay, or the occasional gray whale feeding offshore all invite your immersion in this world at the edge of the sea. The caretakers recommend that guests bring boots, warm clothing, blankets, and if possible, a canoe or kayak—but no pets, motorized recreational vehicles, or loud music. Linens, towels, basic kitchen utensils, and firewood for the woodstove are provided. Write The Ecologic Place, 10 Beach Drive, Nordland 98358, or call (206) 385–3077, for more information.

The ꞈ**Marrowstone Farm House,** located up-island just south of the town of Nordland, offers full use of the oldest and finest Victorian home on the island. Jay Colden, whose family has occupied the house and farmlands for five generations, and partner Cheryl Brunette have restored the 1892 farmhouse with most of its original furnishings and decor, adding modern amenities for convenience and comfort. The farm is set on the top of a hill overlooking Mystery Bay at the island's center. The general store in Nordland is just up the road. The farmhouse is open for guests from March 1 through November 1, and children are welcome. A two-night minimum stay is required. Write to 5034 Flagler Road, Nordland 98358, or call (206) 385–5425, for reservations.

Fort Flagler covers the entire north end of Marrowstone Island with forests, former gun batteries, and rugged coastline. Made obsolete for strategic purposes after the military advances of World War I, the fort was used off and on for military training until it became a park in 1954. Although the campground is busy during the summer (call 206–385–1259 for campsite reservations), the park is big and diverse enough to offer seclusion for those who seek it. Numerous hiking trails go through the forest to cliffs overlooking Admiralty Inlet, where you may see wildlife, such as colorful harlequin ducks feeding offshore or perhaps a peregrine falcon soaring overhead. The **Roots of a Forest** interpretive trail, a short distance past the campground entrance, provides an excellent inside look into forest ecology. There's an indoor interpretive display, open weekends from 1:00 to 4:00 P.M., across from the park office, and a wild, expansive beach to explore at **Marrowstone Point,** down the road at the northeast corner of the park.

The **Ajax Cafe** in Port Hadlock (271 Water Street; 206–385–3450) is an unexpected delight. This unpretentious little restaurant with slightly outrageous decor offers superb dinners, including shark, scallops, salmon, duck, or beef cooked in gourmet sauces. The public wharves, ships, and boatyards across the street add to the ambience. A sign at the dock tells of the history of this now-quiet oceanside spot as a booming industrial site from 1878 to 1916. The cafe is open daily for dinner from 5:00 to 9:00 P.M. and for lunch Friday to Sunday from 11:30 A.M. to 3:30 P.M. Live music begins at 6:00 P.M. daily. Visitors arriving by sea can moor at the Port Hadlock public wharf.

Port Townsend is a fun place to visit. There's plenty to discover, and the community's many art and cultural organizations sponsor festivals, concerts, and conferences. Contact the Port Townsend Chamber of Commerce at 2437 East Sims Way, Port Townsend 98368 (206–385–2722) for event and lodging information. You'll find Port Townsend's downtown packed with small restaurants and shops. Residents enjoy meeting each other and visitors for coffee and delicious sweets at the **Bread and Roses Bakery,** at 230 Quincy Street, or for a fresh, healthy breakfast at the **Salal Cafe,** at 634 Water Street. Both establishments open onto **Franklin Court,** a beautiful courtyard embellished with flowers, wooden walkways, and fruit trees. A narrow passageway past turn-of-the-century brick buildings on Water Street (the main downtown commercial street) between Madison and Quincy streets provides entry into this hidden garden, the site of intimate outdoor concerts. The court is owned and managed by Tom and Lanie Johnson of the **Franklin House**

Gallery, a delightful little gallery at 636 Water Street that features the works of local artists (call 206–385–0620).

The **Jefferson County Historical Museum and Maritime Library,** at Madison and Water streets (206–385–1003), is just northeast of Franklin Court in the town's historic city hall (1891). The four-story museum houses exhibits describing the area's diverse cultural history. You can climb past nautical, native, and Victorian artifacts to the archives on the top story or descend to the basement to see the "dark hole" where the town confined law violators. The museum is open Saturdays from 11:00 A.M. to 4:00 P.M. and Sundays from 1:00 to 4:00 P.M.

Port Townsend has a long and proud nautical tradition that is preserved by an enthusiastic community of craftspeople, sailors, and artists. Follow Water Street northeast until it dead-ends at Point Hudson Marina. There you'll find a strip of shops housing small-boat builders and outfitters that has changed little since the mid-1800s when Port Townsend served as a port of entry to sailing ships from all over the world. This busy harbor was also home to a fishing fleet and a stop for the small working boats that provided transportation around the Sound. Around the marina you can peek into workshops where skilled craftspeople are busy building, repairing, and maintaining traditional boats and nautical gear. The tools, language, and activities hark back hundreds of years, yet there is nothing staged; these people love boats and the ancient skills that keep them working. Give the craftspeople a wide berth when they are busy (shaping a plank or sewing a sail requires concentration), but during a break they will often describe their work with great pride. The final products, beautiful and seaworthy boats, are sitting on display in the marina. If your appetite is whetted by this glimpse into the nautical world, be sure to return during the annual Port Townsend Wooden Boat Festival, held each September when the winds are usually fair.

The **Landfall Restaurant,** at 412 Water Street, is a favorite place to rub shoulders with craftspeople and sailors. The restaurant's large windows overlook the marina, and the informal atmosphere allows easy interaction between locals and visitors. The cuisine is creative but hearty, with a daily special backed up with more conventional omelets and Mexican dishes. Call (206) 385–5814.

Be sure to explore the historic neighborhoods on the hill above downtown Port Townsend. Just follow the stairs up Taylor Street or take either Quincy or Monroe streets up the hill to admire the many Victorian homes that once housed the cultural and financial elite of territorial (pre-statehood) Washington. Stop at the **Old Bell Tower** on Tyler Street on the bluff, which once summoned the volunteer fire department, and see the town's first horse-drawn hearse. One block up and over, at the corner of Jefferson and Taylor streets, you'll find the 1868 ⊃**Rothschild House,** which has been preserved as it was a century ago when it was home to local merchant D.C.H Rothschild, his wife, Dorette, and their five children. The house was donated by the Rothschild family to Washington State in 1959. It is on the National Register of Historic Places and is the smallest park administered by the Washington State Parks and Recreation Commission. Visitors are welcome to tour the house to see the large kitchen, the formal dining room and parlor, and bedrooms filled with original furniture and clothing. Be sure to stroll through the rose garden with its fragrant, many-petaled varieties, some dating back to the sixteenth century and more ancient times. The Rothschild House is open from 11:00 A.M to 4:00 P.M. daily from April 1 to October 1, and holidays and weekends during the off-season.

There are numerous bed and breakfast guest houses scattered among the historic district's many beautiful Victorian homes. Port Townsend offers accommodations for every taste and pocketbook. Make your reservations well in advance for the most popular ones, especially if you visit during the busy summer season. Some lesser-known but still delightful bed and breakfasts are cheaper and in less demand.

If you can't spend a night at the opulent **Ann Starrett Mansion Victorian Bed and Breakfast Inn** (744 Clay Street, Port Townsend 98368), you can still tour the mansion for a small fee between noon and 3:00 P.M. It is a beautiful example of Victorian architecture, complete with octagonal tower, sweeping staircase, and formal sitting rooms. This four-story home was built by George Starrett, a successful contractor, businessman, and mortician, in 1889 for his bride, Ann. The ceiling of the tower is decorated with an eight-panel mural. Four of the mural's panels depict the seasons, and an ingenious mechanism shines a red dot of sunlight on the appropriate panel at midday of each annual solstice and equinox. The decor is charming, the bedrooms comfortable, the food excellent, and the service friendly. For information call (206) 321–3205; for reservations call (800) 321–0644.

Across the street is a less pretentious bed and breakfast that welcomes children and well-mannered pets, and is especially popular with bicyclists and travelers who appreciate a relaxing, homey atmosphere. Robin Shoulberg and Tim Swanson of **Annapurna Inn** (circa 1881) offer nutritious vegetarian breakfasts garnished with fresh fruit from their garden as well as comfortable, sunny rooms, decorated with colorful quilts and curtains. After a day hiking nearby trails, cycling, or walking through town, the innkeepers, (both licensed massage therapists) offer relaxing Swedish or invigorating Sports massage. Contact the Annapurna Inn at 538 Adams, Port Townsend 98368, or call (206) 385–2909.

On a hill south of town is the imposing **Manresa Castle,** at Seventh and Sheridan streets. Built in 1892 by Port Townsend's first mayor, a Prussian baker who made his fortune selling bread and crackers to ships in the harbor, the turreted mansion looks like a medieval castle looming over the city from its hilltop perch. The Jesuit Order that once occupied its rooms named the impressive building after the Spanish town where their order began in the sixteenth century. Now you can splurge there on fancy regional cuisine or stay in one of forty elegant Victorian rooms. Make reservations well in advance as this is a popular spot. Write P.O. Box 564, Port Townsend 98368 or call (800) 732–1281 in Washington or (206) 385–5750 from out of state.

While you are in Port Townsend, be sure to inquire about events at **Fort Worden State Park.** Like Fort Flagler to the east, Fort Worden was once part of the fortifications that protected Puget Sound from sea invasion. Located just 2 miles north of downtown, the fort is the site of many public events organized by the nonprofit Centrum Foundation (P.O. Box 1158, Port Townsend 98368; 206–385–3102). Events include writing, music, and dance conferences, which usually offer activities open to the public. There is also a military museum, nature walks, and a public beach to explore. You can stay in the old barracks or beautiful officers' quarters for special events, in the youth hostel (206–385–0655), or at the campground. For information about vacation housing or camping call (206) 385–4730.

On the dock off the Fort Worden beach is the ⊃**Port Townsend Marine Science Center,** where visitors are encouraged to view sea creatures at close range and handle some of them in "wet tables." Interpretive programs, marine science activities, and summer camps are also offered. Summer hours are noon to 6:00 P.M., Tuesday through Sunday, from June 15 through Labor Day. Other hours are noon to 4:00 P.M. Saturdays and Sundays from Labor Day through October 31 and from March 1 through June 14. The center also is open on Thanksgiving and Christmas weekends. There is a suggested donation of $1.00 for adults and 50 cents for children. Call (206) 385–5582 or (206) 385–4730 for information.

Whidbey Island

Whidbey, the largest of the Puget Sound islands, has been populated for 10,000 years by native people and was one of the first areas on Puget Sound to be settled by Europeans. Its extensive coastline, lush forests, and location midway between the snow-capped Olympic and Cascade mountain ranges create gorgeous views everywhere you look. Whidbey has long been a favorite retreat for city dwellers, offering visitors plenty to do and see. The island retains much of its rural character. Small working farms, artist studios, and innovative home businesses are scattered among evergreen forests. There are several historic communities and small-scale resorts. Whidbey is accessible from the Seattle area and Port Townsend by short ferry rides and from the north across the Deception Pass bridge. To get to Whidbey from the south, take exit 189 (Mukilteo ferry) from Interstate 5 and follow signs through Mukilteo to the ferry slip. Be sure to join the lineup in the right-hand lane. Ferries leave about every half hour and take twenty minutes to reach the island. Call Washington State Ferries at (206) 464–6400 or the statewide toll-free number at (800) 84–FERRY for schedule information.

Highway 525, which becomes Highway 20 north of Keystone, runs down the center of the island, carrying most through traffic. We recommend that you take the meandering local roads that follow the shoreline for better views and less traffic. Many visitors to Whidbey choose to leave cars on the mainland. This avoids delays waiting for vehicle space on a ferry and provides an intimate way to experience the landscape. You can take bicycles on the ferry or rent them at several island bike shops. You can also use the free Island Transit bus service; call (206) 678–7771 for information. Residents appreciate visitors who leave their cars off-island, minimizing traffic and other environmental problems.

Langley, the "Village by the Sea" on Saratoga Passage, is a favorite community to visit. To get there, turn right on Langley Road off Highway 525 and follow signs into town. On the way, you can visit **Blackfish Studio and Gallery** at 5075 South Langley Road (206–321–1274). There you can view Donald Miller's award-winning photographs and Kathleen Miller's exquisite hand-painted silk and wool garments. Kathleen is often at work in the sunny studio, and the artists are always happy to talk with visitors.

Langley has many antique and art galleries and a variety of places to eat. Although a busy tourist town during summer week-ends, it is always pleasant, with plenty of spots to sit and view the magnificent scenery or the browsing shoppers. You'll want to join Georgia Gerber's bronze statue on First Street of a sea-gazing boy leaning over the railing above Saratoga Passage, with his dog lying at his side. From there a wooden staircase leads down to the beach, where you can stroll along a grassy walkway or descend farther to the pebbly shore below a bulkhead sculpted with images of salmon and whales.

You'll find cafes, restaurants, espresso bars, and bistros to suit every taste on First and Second streets. For a Mediterranean treat, try the Garibyan Brothers' ⊃**Langley Cafe.** In a cheery room filled with natural light and decorated with scenes of the sea, you can enjoy lamb or garbanzo delights wrapped in fresh pita bread for lunch, generous servings of shish kebab for dinner, and delicious baclava for dessert. The cafe, at 113 First Street (206–221–3090), is open for lunch from 11:30 A.M. to 2:30 P.M. and for dinner from 5:00 to 8:30 P.M. The **Childers/Proctor Gallery** (302 First Street; 206–221–2978) presents the work of established regional artists. The gallery also has a single beautiful suite overlooking Saratoga Passage for overnight stays with a deli-cious continental breakfast. **The Clyde Theater,** also on First Street, offers contemporary films and occasional live theater pro-ductions, Wednesday through Sunday evenings. For live enter-tainment on Saturday evenings, try the **Raven Cafe,** at 197 Second Avenue (206–221–3211). The Raven features jazz, folk, and country music by local musicians. The cafe, with imposing raven dance masks in its wide-windowed front room, offers gourmet pizzas, vegetarian soups, deli sandwiches, espresso, and fresh juices from 7:00 A.M. to 5:00 P.M. weekdays, 8:00 A.M. till late Saturdays, and 9:00 A.M. to 3:00 P.M. Sundays.

Langley is home to the **Giraffe Project,** a national nonprofit organization that gives public recognition to individuals who, like giraffes, stick their necks out to make the world a better place. It focuses on people who work quietly, to demonstrate that an individual can make a difference. The small storefront office next to the Raven Cafe, open during regular business hours, offers information packets and sells giraffe T-shirts and mugs to help support the organization. For more information contact the Giraffe Project, P.O. Box 759, Langley 98206, or call (206) 221–7989.

There are a plethora of bed and breakfasts to choose from in the area. The **Twickenham House Bed and Breakfast Inn** (5023 Langley Road, Langley 98260; 800–874–5009), on the road from the ferry dock to Langley, is a quiet ten-acre country retreat surrounded by sheep pastures. All rooms have private baths and covered access to the main house. Hosts Maureen and Ray Cooke pamper visitors with excellent breakfasts, tasteful accommodations (including a gallery of local artists' work), and gracious hospitality. The **Strawbridge Inn Bed and Breakfast** (4667 Strawbridge Lane, Langley 98260; 206–321–6567) is a secluded turn-of-the-century beachfront farmhouse within walking distance of downtown Langley. Rooms feature antique furniture and views of Saratoga Passage. The Strawbridge Inn welcomes children. The **Blue House Inn** (513 Anthes, Langley 98260; 206–221–8392) is a cozy, relaxed home in Langley. Families will appreciate **Uncle John's Cottage** (1762 East Lancaster Road, Freeland 98249; 206–321–7129). There are two comfortable furnished cottages on a quiet farm complete with hammock, swing, children's toys, barbecue, and hot tub. You'll find the kitchen stocked with delicious items to prepare a hearty breakfast at your leisure.

Whidbey Island has long attracted visitors who enjoy fishing. There were once a dozen fishing resorts, mostly along the west shore, where families vacationed, but over the past two decades most have been converted to upscale establishments or private homes. **Bush Point Resort** off Bush Point Road on Admiralty Inlet retains the informal character of the older resorts. Packs of barefoot kids enjoy ice cream at the Bush Point Mercantile, parents "drift mooch" (a popular low-effort fishing technique) in small boats at the spit, and the smell of barbecued salmon wafts among campers. For information contact Bush Point Resort at 326 South Main Street, Freeland 98249, or call (206) 321–1824.

The rhododendron, Washington's state flower, is especially prolific on Whidbey Island. You'll see many beautiful samples growing wild or used for landscaping. If these pique your interest you'll want to visit **Meerkerk Rhododendron Gardens.** The colorful trumpet-shaped rhododendron blooms are usually at their peak the last two weeks of April and the beginning of May, but Meerkerk Gardens are lovely at any time. Willed to the Seattle Rhododendron Society by owner Ann Meerkerk, the garden features over 800 mature rhododendron and companion plants and a wide variety of new hybrids. The forested landscape includes ponds, forest and seaside nature trails, and wooden benches for sitting and contemplating the serene environment. To get there, turn east off Highway 525 on Resort Road, 1½ miles south of Greenbank, or follow the scenic Honeymoon Bay Road for 5 miles north from Freeland along Holmes Harbor. For more information call (206) 678–8740 or 321–6682.

Hillsides covered with vines at the historic **Greenbank Loganberry Farm** are a pleasant setting for a picnic, and visitors are welcome to tour the farm where loganberries (a raspberry/blackberry cross) are distilled into a popular liqueur. This is the only place where you can purchase Whidbey's Loganberry Liqueur, and connoisseurs have been known to travel across the country just to obtain a personal supply. The gift shop sells snacks for your picnic basket in addition to samples. The farm, on Wonn Road off Highway 525, a quarter mile north of Greenbank, is open daily from 10:00 A.M. to 4:30 P.M. For information call (206) 678–7700.

An ideal way to visit historic **Coupeville** is by private yacht or aboard the Mosquito Fleet steamboat *Spirit of Saratoga Passage* on its way to Deception Pass. Call (206) 252–6800 for more information on Puget Sound Mosquito Fleet tours. Sailing into the security of Penn Cove, you'll see the cluster of buildings that constitute the town clinging to the hillside like barnacles to a rock. There are excellent anchorage and public docking facilities. Coupeville's maritime hospitality is no accident. It was founded in the 1850s by several sailing-era sea captains—including Captain Thomas Coupe, for whom the town is named—who were seeking a pleasant and secure place to settle ashore. Coupeville is also a fun place to visit for those who arrive by land. There are plenty of places to eat, sleep, and explore. You can easily imagine being an old salt of bygone years on shore leave. The community has the intimate air of a New England town, with many carefully preserved homes dating from the nineteenth century and a waterfront crowded with lively entertainment.

Coupeville's **All Island Bicycles** (302 North Main Street; 202–678–3351) rents bicycles—including mountain bikes, tandems, child trailers, and helmets—and offers maps of favorite bicycling routes on the island. Owner Peter Gnehm will go out of his way to ensure that everybody has an enjoyable experience.

The ꙨIsland County Historical Museum, at the end of Front Street by the wharf, has beautiful displays describing local native and pioneer life. Outside are examples of sleek eleven-paddler Indian dugout racing canoes. You are welcome to touch the detailed semi-relief carving on the front doors depicting activities of earlier days. Inside you'll find exhibits of tribal life, a pioneer cabin, models of boats and ships that sailed Puget Sound, and an extensive collection of historic photos. The museum is open Tuesday through Sunday from 11:00 A.M. to 5:00 P.M. Call (206) 678–3310 for more information. Pick up the "A Walk Through History" brochure at the museum which describes an enjoyable walking tour of Coupeville, with information on more than two dozen historic buildings. Most have been carefully preserved and renovated, including many of the old commercial buildings on Front Street that are still in use. The **Knead & Feed Restaurant** (206–678–5431), a former storehouse and laundry built in 1871 near Main Street, is nestled one level down the bluff under the Tartan and Tweed Store. Its original post-and-beam structure adds to the ambience of this pleasant, seaside spot. A full-time baker makes breads and desserts daily, and the restaurant's homemade soups are excellent.

Coupeville offers a wide variety of overnight accommodations. Both the **Inn at Penn Cove** (702 North Main, Coupeville 98239; 800–688–COVE) and **The Victorian** (602 North Main Street, Coupeville 98239; 206–678–5305) bed and breakfasts are located in carefully renovated Victorian houses. Guests enjoy the charming ambience of these historic homes while indulging in modern comforts and gracious hospitality. The **Captain Whidbey Inn** (2072 West Whidbey Island Inn Road, Coupeville 98239; 206–678–4097) has served as a pleasant retreat on the shore of Penn Cove since it was built in 1907 by Judge Lester Still. Visitors once traveled from Seattle by paddle steamer to enjoy the quiet surroundings and warm hospitality. Many visitors still arrive by boat, and the quiet and warmth offered at the resort hasn't changed. The lodge, built of madrona logs, has comfortable rooms, good food, a cozy beachstone fireplace, and the Chart Room bar. To get there from Coupeville, follow scenic Madrona Way for 3 miles along Penn Cove, then turn right at the sign.

Whidbey Island beaches were an important Indian camping area for thousands of years before Europeans arrived in the 1850s. Much of the western shoreline along the center of Whidbey Island has been preserved as a National Historical Reserve. There are old forts to explore, long stretches of undeveloped public beaches, and major tracts of protected forest and farmland. ⊃**Ebey's Landing National Historical Reserve** was established by Congress in 1978 as the first such reserve in the nation. The reserve allows landowners and government agencies to cooperate in order to preserve historic buildings, farmland, and public access. It includes over 17,000 acres of land, 90 percent of which is in private ownership. Follow the trail from the small parking lot off Ebey's Landing Road up the windswept Prairie Bluff for a spectacular view of Puget Sound and the Olympic Mountains. You'll see mountains to the west and, to the east, farms that are little changed since the first settlers established homesteads in the 1850s. In clear weather you'll catch a glimpse of Mount Rainier and the Cascade Mountains on the mainland. From the top of the bluff you can hike to the Sunnyside Cemetery, where many of the original pioneers are buried.

The beauty of Deception Pass at Whidbey's north end is incredible. On busy summer weekends, so are the crowds. For a different view of the Deception Pass State Park area, we recommend a stop at the **Civilian Conservation Corps (CCC) Interpretive Center** just south of Pass Lake on the Fidalgo Island side of the park. Here you'll gain insight into the park's history and the young men of the lean Depression years who made the trails and hewed the distinctive railings and other park structures by hand. The best way to see the pass is from the water. The Mosquito Fleet (206–252–6800) offers a splendid cruise up Saratoga Passage from Everett through the steep canyon walls of Deception Pass, with a stop at Coupeville along the way.

Anacortes

Just across the dramatic Deception Pass bridge from Whidbey Island is Fidalgo Island. For a bird's-eye view of this island, turn west from Highway 20 just south of Pass Lake (en route to the CCC Interpretive Center) and follow Rosario Road as it forks right, away from Burrows Bay. At the Lake Erie Grocery take an acute left onto Heart Lake Road, then turn right to enter **Mount Erie Park.** The steep road (not recommended for trailers or RVs) has several trails and observation points along the way, and the vista from the 1,300-foot summit is spectacular. North Puget Sound stretches out beneath your perch on the mountain's rocky outcroppings amid sweet pine scents. Continue right on Heart Lake Road to reach the town of **Anacortes,** through which San Juan Islands ferry traffic passes. Many tourists are in such a hurry to catch their boat that they never take time to explore this eclectic community. Anacortes also makes a great base camp where you can leave your bags and car to explore the San Juan Islands on day trips by ferry, bus, bicycle, or foot.

Anacortes has a historic downtown area along North Commercial Avenue. You will see ship chandlers (nautical supply stores) and other specialty businesses serving the marine industries scattered among newer art galleries, cafes, and boutiques. On many street corners you'll find colorful, life-size cutouts of the town's pioneers, from Anacortes' namesake, Annie Curtis, between Eighth and Ninth streets, to the town's first safety bicycle on Third Street. One block east at Sixth Street and Q Avenue, you can see the **W. T. Preston,** the "last of the Puget Sound sternwheelers," which worked until the early 1980s. In a land of loggers and water traffic, this hard-working "snagboat" and champion racer fulfilled the important function of clearing log jams that formed on Puget Sound's vital waterways. The *Preston* is open for viewing from 11:00 A.M. to 5:00 P.M., Friday through Sunday.

⊃**The Majestic** (419 Commercial Avenue, Anacortes 98221; 206–293–3355), built in 1889 and recently reopened after six years of careful renovation, is a luxurious hotel. Located at the heart of the historic district at Commercial and Fifth, the Majestic offers twenty-three individually decorated rooms featuring European antiques as well as modern amenities, a cozy library, an English garden, and a rooftop cupola with 360-degree views of

North Puget Sound. Within its walls you can enjoy fine lunches and dinners and an elegant Sunday brunch served from 9:00 A.M. to 2:30 P.M. **Gere-a-Deli** (502 Commercial Avenue; 206–293–7383), catercorner to the Majestic, offers light homemade meals in an open, community-oriented setting from 8:00 A.M. to 5:00 P.M. Monday through Saturday.

You'll find interesting sights in the older neighborhoods just west of Commercial Avenue on Sixth through Twelfth streets. **Causland Memorial Park,** on Eighth Street between M and N avenues, is a pleasant green hideaway surrounded by mosaic walls made of white quartz and red argillite swirling in brown and gray sandstone. John LePage, a French-Canadian architect, designed the park in 1919 to honor citizens killed in World War I. Across the street you can review the history of Fidalgo Island at the **Anacortes Museum** (1350 Eighth Street), once the town's Carnegie Library. Several blocks west is the **Blue Rose Bed and Breakfast** (1811 Ninth Street, Anacortes 98221; 206–293–5175), a friendly, country-style bungalow built in 1910 and featuring delicious breakfasts and beautiful views.

For a pleasant drive or bicycle ride take Twelfth Avenue westward past the ferry exit. Follow Sunset Avenue onto Loop Road around **Washington Park,** where you'll find access to several public beaches. At Fidalgo Head you'll enjoy a magnificent viewpoint on a high promontory overlooking Burrows Island and Bay. Circle back to Sunset Drive, then turn right at Skyline, left at Kingsway, and right at MacBeth to find **A Burrow's Bay Bed and Breakfast** (4911 MacBeth, Anacortes 98221), a cozy home offering spectacular views from a wide wooden deck overlooking the San Juans. Call (206) 293–4792 for reservations.

Fertile Valleys

The Skagit and Nooksack Valleys are flat and fertile, filled with traditional family farms. During April many fields explode with a vivid rainbow of tulips and daffodils, which thrive in the rich loamy soil of the Lower Skagit Valley. Fields of these joyful springtime flowers are visible from most roadways. Views of snow-capped Mount Baker in the distance frame the scene. Tulips and bulbs are sold at roadside stands, and visitors may tour some of these happy fields. Call (800) 4–TULIPS or (206) 428–8547 for information on the annual Skagit Valley Tulip Festival in April.

The low, flat delta land of the Skagit River forms Fir Island. The island is divided between fertile flower and vegetable farms and the **Skagit Wildlife Area,** which supports fox, deer, and a huge bird population. There is always something for visitors to see. During the winter, flocks of snow geese browse over the frozen farmland. In spring, the colorful tapestry of flowers makes Fir Island a popular tourist attraction. Summer is a busy time for local farmers, and visitors can enjoy a variety of summer berries. In autumn, truck farms provide an abundance of fresh produce, much of which is sold at roadside stands. The **White Swan Guest House** (1388 Moore Road, Mount Vernon 98273; 206–445–6805) offers cozy accommodations amidst the island's beauty. The restored 1890s farmhouse, "just like Grandma's house," has three guest rooms, a big porch, a wood stove, and colorful gardens. For greater privacy try the Garden Cottage, a separate little house ideal for families with children or a romantic retreat. Owner Peter Goldfarb provides generous hospitality, including cookies fresh from the kitchen.

Just north of Fir Island at 1935 Chillberg Road is **Pleasant Ridge Pottery and Gallery** (206–446–4592), a charming haven of locally produced pottery, jewelry, clothing, and woodwork. The atmosphere is colorful and tasteful, showing the beautifully crafted goods at their best. Even the display shelves are skillfully assembled with wood pegs. Then follow Chillberg Road west to **La Conner,** which sits on the bank of the Swinomish Channel, or slough, a natural canal that carries a colorful parade of small boats between Padilla Bay to the north and Skagit Bay to the south. Once a quiet village serving local farmers and fishermen, La Conner is now a popular tourist destination, with restaurants, antique shops, and boutiques clustered along First Street overlooking Swinomish Channel. On summer weekends crowds descend on this small community, so if possible visit on a weekday or off-season. Be sure to climb the hill to the ⊃**Skagit County Museum** at 501 Fourth Street, which includes exhibits on the area's history, industries, and fashions. The museum is open from 1:00 to 5:00 P.M. Wednesday through Sunday and charges a small admission fee. Call (206) 466–3365 for more information.

Head north from La Conner on Whitney-La Conner Road and cross Highway 20 onto Bayview Edison Road, which offers beautiful views of the offshore islands and marine wildlife of **Padilla**

Bay. If you have time, walk or bicycle along the 2.5-mile Padilla Bay Shore Trail. You'll pass Bay View State Park, Padilla Bay National Estuarine Wildlife Research Reserve, and ⊃**Breazeale Interpretive Center.** The center is a fascinating educational facility that makes learning about the environment fun for children of all ages. In addition to fish tanks and displays of local birds and mammals, you can enjoy environmental games and hands-on activities. The center even lends binoculars for bird-watching along the reserve's beach and trails. Because of its fertile waters, Padilla Bay is a major stop for migrating birds. Breazeale is open year round from 10:00 A.M. to 5:00 P.M. Wednesday through Sunday. For information on upcoming events, contact the center at 1043 Bayview-Edison Road, Mount Vernon 98273, or call (206) 428–1558.

Continuing north, the road passes through more farmland on the Samish River delta, crosses the river, and joins Highway 237 into the community of Edison. Stop at the **Samish Fine Art Studio,** where you'll encounter the beautiful handiwork of the local artist community, including sculpture, pottery, and fabric arts. If the studio is closed, you may be able to drop in on the artists in their workshops; directions are posted on the studio door. Across the street is **Samish Island Art Glass,** where you might find a stained-glass work that just fits your needs or, if not, have one commissioned.

Where Highway 237 crosses Highway 11 (Chuckanut Drive), you will find one of the unexpected gastronomic delights of this area, the **Rhododendron Cafe** (206–766–6667). Although modest on the outside and informal inside, this 35-seat restaurant offers excellent food and service that attract visitors from all over the region to enjoy "country fare with a flair." Fresh Northwest cuisine is highlighted, including plenty of seafood, locally grown vegetables, fruits and berries, and a selection of basic hearty dishes to satisfy farmers and fishermen.

Across the street is the **Chuckanut Valley Store,** a local hangout and an emporium of old or interesting knickknacks. The antique barber's chair is an inviting spot to sit and drink coffee from the ever-brewing pot, where you'll hear news and gossip from local residents. A few miles south, the old **Benson Farmstead** bed and breakfast (1009 Avon-Allen Road, Bow 98232; 206–757–0578) stands three stories tall amidst green fields. The building is brimming with antique decor. Every morning the big farm kitchen produces terrific smells and hearty breakfasts. This is one of the few bed and breakfasts in the area that welcomes children. A delightful playground with climbing toys and sandbox beckons beyond the English garden out back.

Once you get away from the shopping malls along Interstate 5, **Bellingham** is a wonderful city to explore, full of historical and cultural surprises. Many of the city's old commercial and residential buildings have been renovated to their nineteenth-century grandeur, especially in the **Fairhaven District** and downtown Bellingham. To reach Fairhaven take Interstate 5 exit 250 and follow Highway 11 west to Twelfth Street. In addition to wandering around the shopping district, you'll want to explore the waterfront, which includes the new Alaska Ferry terminal. From Fairhaven you can follow Twelfth Street north (it becomes State Street) to downtown Bellingham, or take Interstate 5 exit 254.

The **Whatcom Museum of History and Art** (206–676–6981), in the beautiful Old City Hall at 121 Prospect, is a good place to start your explorations. The museum is open noon to 5:00 P.M. Tuesday through Sunday, and admission is free. You can pick up a walking map of the downtown or follow the multi-colored footprints from the museum along the route of the Uptown Gallery Walk, which is held several evenings each summer. For information on this popular event contact Lewis Wallach, P.O. Box 1175, Bellingham 98227–1175, or call (206) 733–7847. Many of Bellingham's charming old houses are open for overnight guests. Contact the Bed and Breakfast Guild of Whatcom County at (206) 676–4560 for a list of options.

If you hanker for the nautical adventure of a lifetime, consider sailing on the **Schooner *Zodiac*,** a beautiful 127-foot retired pilot boat that has been carefully renovated by volunteers to her original beauty. Now listed on the National Register of Historic Places, the *Zodiac* cruises Puget Sound on trips from one to six days, carrying up to forty-nine guests in addition to a full crew. For information about her sailing schedule call (206) 325–6122 or write P.O. Box 322, Snohomish 98290.

Ferndale is a great place to explore both history and nature. Even the town's name comes from the fern-covered terrain described by the area's first teacher, in the mid-1800s. Within walking distance of the town's main street are several wonderful places to visit. Two blocks south of Main Street on First Avenue you'll find **Pioneer Park,** home to the largest collection of nineteenth-century log structures in the state. You can tour these sturdy buildings, hewn from the giant cedars that once covered the Northwest, from noon to 5:00 P.M. May 1 through September 30.

Housed in the restored turn-of-the-century Nielsen Farmhouse, the ⊃**Tennant Lake Natural History Interpretive Center** provides an excellent background to the vital wetland environment surrounding Tennant Lake. Visitors to the center are in for a sensory treat. The front yard of this 1906 farmhouse overflows with a "fragrance garden," herbs and flowers chosen for their rich colors, aromas, and textures. You are invited to gently touch and smell the leaves of delightful plants such as curry, gingermint, chamomile, lavender, sage, or woolly thyme. The garden is wheelchair-accessible, and braille signs are posted on the inside of the handrails. A gardener is available most weekdays to answer questions; call the center to arrange a special tour. You can walk along the half-mile system of boardwalks, bridges, and reed-lined paths through the surrounding marshlands in any season and see a wide variety of raptors and waterfowl, including large flocks of trumpeter swans in winter. To get to the center from town, turn right off Main Street (after crossing the Nooksack River and just before going under the railroad trestle) onto Hovander Drive, then follow the signs. The center is open from mid-June to mid-September, Thursday through Sunday, noon to 6:00 P.M. Call (206) 384–3444 for more information or to arrange a tour.

You'll find another great destination by following the marked, half-mile path from Tennant Lake to **Hovander Homestead Park** (5299 Nielsen Road; 206–384–3444). This family mansion was built in 1896 by Hakan Hovander, a talented Swedish architect who created many fine buildings in his homeland and helped rebuild Chicago after the Great Fire of 1871. The Hovander House has been carefully restored to its original beauty. Volunteers in period clothing will show you through the elegant rooms from noon to 4:30 P.M. on Saturdays and Sundays in May, and Thursday through Sunday from June through Labor Day. There are farm animals on the grounds in summer and antique farm equipment at the big red barn, as well as a demonstration garden outside the homestead with information on setting up your own home compost system or creating a raised-bed vegetable garden. On the park's 200 well-cared-for acres you'll find hayfields, orchards, walking trails, river views, playground equipment, and picnic tables. You can also experience traditional Scottish fun when the park hosts the Bellingham Highland Games in June or enjoy some of the world's best dance bands at the International Folkdance Festival in July.

Dave Anderson leads 10-kilometer "volksmarches" to many of Ferndale's parks and sites from his **Anderson House Bed and Breakfast** (2140 Main Street, Ferndale 98248; 206–384–3450). Situated on a hill overlooking town, with snow-capped Mount Baker beyond, this 1897 home offers a warm, tranquil respite from the twentieth century. The **Douglas House** restaurant, built in 1904, is nearby at 2254 Douglas Drive (206–384–5262) and serves lunch from 11:30 A.M. to 2:00 P.M. and dinner from 5:00 to 9:00 P.M. Wednesday through Saturday; Sunday brunch is from 11:00 A.M. to 3:00 P.M. **Slater Heritage House Bed and Breakfast,** located a mile east of the Ferndale exit from Interstate 5 (1371 West Axton Road, Ferndale 98248; 206–384–4273), is another fine turn-of-the-century retreat.

Perched on a hill overlooking lush dairy farms, **Lynden** is a friendly community with a hospitable downtown and a proud Dutch heritage. Set in the fertile Nooksack Valley farmlands, Lynden was once the largest Dutch settlement in the state. Stroll down Front Street, bedecked with flowers and quaint Dutch decor, and stop in for a fresh Dutch Marine roll at the **Lynden Dutch Bakery** or authentic European cuisine at **Dutch Mothers** restaurant (206–354–2174). If you arrive in town in early May for Holland days, you'll see a reenactment of Dutch tradition when costumed townspeople scrub down the streets.

The ‹**Lynden Pioneer Museum,** at 217 Front Street (206–354–3675), offers visitors a chance to explore the community's past. You can stroll through a re-created turn-of-the-century main street, with stores, cafe, doctor and dentist offices, school, church, and train station. There are displays of Northwest Indian artifacts, historic household goods, early cars, over 40 restored horse buggies and wagons, and antique farm machinery. Much of the farm equipment is still operating. In spring you can watch huge draft horses working at the International Plowing Match, and in midsummer you'll see steam tractors and threshing machines in action at the Puget Sound Antique Tractor and Machinery Association's Threshing Bee.

The **Century House Bed and Breakfast,** built as a homestead in 1888 and fully restored a hundred years later, offers an

71

elegant Victorian retreat. All rooms have been furnished with antiques and tastefully decorated. Guests have a choice of the third-floor Century Tower Suite, which offers exceptional views of the valley and Cascade Mountains; the Garden View Room, with a red floral theme; and the Rose Room, decorated in relaxing muted colors. Hosts Jan and Ken Stremler offer gracious hospitality. The Century House can be contacted at 401 South B.C. Avenue, Lynden 98264 (206–354–2439).

San Juan Islands

The San Juan Islands, a popular vacation spot, are an exquisite conjunction of inland waters, rolling farmland, dramatic natural geologic formations, and charming communities. Islanders are famous for their friendliness. It also doesn't hurt that the San Juans are in the rain shadow of the Olympic Mountains and receive more sun than other coastal areas.

Almost everybody loves to visit the San Juans, a fact that creates several problems. Too many visitors can strain the resources and hospitality of the islands' small communities and crowd the natural features that make the islands so attractive. Some residents want to discourage more tourism, and everybody wants to reduce the impacts of accommodating so many visitors. Here are some tips for an enjoyable and responsible visit to these islands:

- Avoid visiting during the busy tourist season. The islands have much to offer in autumn, winter, and spring, and you will avoid being "one of the crowd."
- If possible, leave your car behind. These islands are ideal for bicycling, kayaking, or walking. By using human-powered travel, you minimize impacts on the land and experience a more intimate relationship with island environments. Before taking a ferry like the *Kaleetah* over to the islands, you can rent a bicycle at the **Ship Harbor Bicycle Rental** (800–852–8568 or 206–293–5177), a quarter-mile from the ferry terminal in Anacortes at 5316 Ferry Terminal Road. There are also small bike rental shops on San Juan, Orcas, and Lopez islands.
- Don't waste water. All of the islands face water shortages.
- Don't rush. Island residents are proud to live on "island time," which means that there is always time to be neighborly. They are annoyed with visitors who bring impatient habits from the

The *Kaleetah*

mainland. When you've arrived in Paradise, islanders point out, there is no need to hurry.

As you drive or bicycle on these islands, you may be surprised that other drivers offer a friendly wave as they pass. This is an old tradition from the days when the islands were so isolated that every encounter, even passing on the roadway, was worth acknowledging. This tradition is still common on Lopez and Shaw and certainly worth supporting.

All four islands with regular ferry service—Lopez, Shaw, Orcas, and San Juan—offer plenty to explore. Lopez and Shaw islands are the most off the beaten path. Shaw, the smallest San Juan island accessible by public ferry, offers a pleasant step back in time. Franciscan Sisters run the ferry dock and the adjacent ⊃**Little Portion General Store.** This is the only place on Shaw to buy provisions, so stock up there for a picnic. The charming old store also features gift items handmade by various religious orders, including herb vinegars, sachets, and spices prepared by the Shaw Island Franciscan Service. Old baskets, fruit boxes, and nautical paraphernalia decorate the walls.

The **Shaw Island Public Library,** in the center of the island on Blind Bay Road, is a delightful spot for quiet reflection. It's a beautiful, sunny little building, open 2:00 to 4:00 P.M. Tuesdays and Saturdays, and 10:00 A.M. to noon on Thursdays. Inside, the smell of cedar fills the air as you sit back in a cozy spot with a good book and a view of the surrounding forest. The children's corner is full of old favorites and new stories around a colorful rug peppered with pillows and child-size chairs. If it's not too busy, the volunteer librarian may share stories about Shaw Island's history and open up the historic cabin around the corner. Opposite the library is the schoolyard. The old red schoolhouse is over one hundred years old. A new school was built in the 1980s for the island's small number of elementary students.

Head south along Hoffman Cove Road, then left on Squaw Bay Road past secluded Squaw Bay. Past the bay is the turnoff to **South Beach Park,** with several campsites overlooking the sea. The small beach provides a quiet picnic spot with ample supplies of driftwood logs for rustic benches in the sand. From here, follow Squaw Bay Road through a beautiful valley back to Blind Bay and the ferry dock.

Lopez Island is larger and more developed than Shaw but still offers many opportunities for quiet and seclusion. Lopez village, with a museum, store, and three restaurants, is the island's commercial center. The ꓷ**Lopez Historical Museum,** full of island history and lore, is worth a stop. The museum is open Friday to Sunday, 12:00 to 4:00 P.M. Call (206) 468-2049 for more information. Don't miss **Holly's Bakery** (open spring through fall), a favorite with bicyclists. **Gail's Deli and Catering** features delicious omelets and waffles, fresh muffins, cinnamon rolls, and a wide selection of Seattle's Starbucks coffee. **Edenwild Inn** (P.O. Box 271, Lopez 98261; 206-468-3238) offers family-style breakfasts and accommodations with garden and water views within walking distance of town. If you're looking for something closer to the water, **Mackaye Harbor Inn** (P.O. Box 1940, Lopez 98261; 206-468-2253), a Victorian bed and breakfast, offers elegant beachfront accommodations. The inn provides guests with guided kayak trips as well as bicycle and boat rentals.

Lovely public beaches on Lopez Island include the west side of **Fisherman Bay** off Bay Shore Road, **Shark Reef Park** at the end of Shark Reef Road on the island's southwest tip, and **Agate Beach** off Mackaye Harbor Road at the island's south end. **Spencer Spit State Park** on the island's east shore is a beautiful, rugged spot. Campsites are situated on the forested hill above a long, sandy spit reaching out into the channel. The constant action of tides and waves make this a dynamic geologic formation.

Traveling around the fields, shores, and forests of Lopez and Shaw, you will appreciate why islanders are so concerned about preserving the integrity of the island environment. Several nonprofit organizations have made it their mission to conserve the open spaces still left. The San Juan Preservation Trust, located on Lopez Island, has helped set aside more than 2,000 acres since it began its work over a decade ago. For more information, contact the trust at P.O. Box 327, Lopez 98261, or call (206) 468-3202.

Point Roberts

U.S. and British soldiers spent thirteen years in a standoff on San Juan Island following the 1846 decision to divide their common territory along the 49th parallel. Britain got the southernmost tip of Vancouver Island that extends below the 49th parallel, while the San Juan Islands and a little peninsula that hangs below the 49th parallel south of British Columbia became U.S. territory. ꓛ**Point Roberts** peninsula is accessible from the rest of Washington state by boat or by driving into British Columbia on Highway 99, then east on Highway 17 toward the ferry docks, then south through Tsawwassen, B.C. Point Roberts is a quiet community popular with Canadian retirees and vacationers.

Bicycling is a great way to explore the area. You can rent one from Steve Dyde at the **Happy Cyclist's Bike Shop,** 1347-A Gulf Road. Call (206) 945-0686 to ensure that bikes, helmets, and child seats will be ready when you need them. It's an easy jaunt from the bike shop to **Lighthouse Marine Park** (811 Marine Drive; 206-945-4911) at the peninsula's southwest corner. The windswept park has plenty of camping and picnic sites adjacent to the beach. A thirty-foot wooden tower above the boardwalk offers great views of Georgia Strait.

The **Point Roberts Marina** (206-945-2255), at the south end of Tyee Drive, is a haven for boaters. Landlubbers can get a close-up look at vessels hauled out of the water for maintenance and stop for a snack at the **Dockside Cafe** (206–945–1206). A fine place to have dinner while still taking in the beautiful views is the **South Beach House,** east of the marina at 725 South Beach Road. Wednesday through Sunday from 5:30 P.M. on, this pleasant seaside restaurant features ling cod, lamb, and polenta as well as vegetables stir-fried to perfection before your eyes on an open Mongolian barbecue. Call (206) 945–0717 for reservations.

Off the Beaten Path in Northcentral Washington

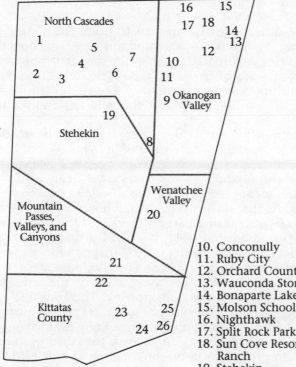

North Cascades

1
5
4
2 3 6 7

19

Stehekin

8

16 15
17 18
14
13
12
10
11

9 Okanogan Valley

Wenatchee Valley
20

Mountain Passes, Valleys, and Canyons

21
22

Kittatas County
23 25
24 26

1. Baker Lake
2. Cascade Mountain Inn
3. Cascadian Farm Organic Market
4. Seattle City Light Visitor Center
5. Ross Lake Resort
6. Washington Pass Overlook
7. Mazama Country Inn
8. Amy's Manor
9. Okanogan County Historical Museum

10. Conconully
11. Ruby City
12. Orchard Country Inn
13. Wauconda Store and Cafe
14. Bonaparte Lake Resort
15. Molson School
16. Nighthawk
17. Split Rock Park
18. Sun Cove Resort and Guest Ranch
19. Stehekin
20. Douglas County Historical Museum
21. Liberty
22. The Moore House Bed and Breakfast
23. Murphy's Country Bed and Breakfast
24. Lower Yakima River Canyon
25. Ginkgo Petrified Forest State Park
26. Wanapum Dam Visitor's Center

Northcentral Washington

The forces of nature show little restraint in forming Northcentral Washington terrain. Pressures deep underground created by the movement of our continent have caused buckling and folding on a massive scale, raising huge chunks of granite—the Earth's bones—miles into the air and forming the Cascade Mountain range. We're talking *big* mountains here, big enough to make visitors tingle with excitement at the spectacular beauty and superhuman scale of the landscape. The Cascades give visitors a humbling reminder that we are only human on a large, dynamic, and wonderful planet that still has a mind of its own.

These mountain-building activities are countered by the steady flow of water, the accumulated strength of individual raindrops and the weight of single snowflakes. Rivers cascade down steep mountain sides, cutting canyons and valleys that create riparian (riverside) environments. Nothing is more refreshing than to see, hear, feel, and taste the water of a lively mountain stream. If the water is turquoise-gray, it originates from one of the Cascades' many active glaciers, unstoppable rivers of ice that scour the land, moving boulders and creating wide U-shaped valleys.

Abundant water, rich volcanic soil, and hot summers make the Okanogan, Chelan, and Wenatchee river valleys on the east side of the Cascade range ideal for fruit growing. The sunshine of eastern Washington is caught, one photon at a time, and converted by trees, vines, and bushes into increasingly complex sugars to delight your palate. Many visitors leave with cases of fruits and vegetables to preserve as a future reminder of this earthly Eden or a few bottles from one of the small wineries. Depending on the season you'll find cherries, apples, pears, peaches, corn, and field-ripened vegetables. Fresh tomatoes picked ripe and juicy from the vine are alone worth a pilgrimage.

Farther east, the landscape mellows into dry, scrub-covered hills. You can explore back roads, ghost towns, and a scattering of small and friendly lakeside fishing resorts. Okanogan and North Cascades national forests offer thousands of miles of trails, making it easy to hike, cross-country ski, trail ride, or mountain bike your way off the beaten path.

North Cascades

The North Cascades are truly spectacular mountains, covered with emerald-green forests and cut by rivers, waterfalls, and lakes whose frigid turquoise waters show their glacial origins. Cloud-covered peaks tease visitors with glimpses of towering summits. Once at the bottom of an ancient sea, today's mountains were forged into magnificent spires and horn-shaped peaks. Ancient glaciers carved the U-shaped valleys that separate the peaks, and many high mountain recesses remain entombed year-round in blue ice. You can see forested slopes strangely carved by green avalanche chutes, the result of the heavy snowpack that covers much of the range in winter.

Approaching from the west, you'll see lush forests of western red cedar, Douglas fir, and western hemlock richly carpeted with the moss and ferns that thrive on the abundant moisture on the Pacific side of the Cascade Crest. At the timberline between 4,500 and 5,500 feet elevation, beautiful alpine meadows painted with brightly colored wildflowers and rugged outcroppings sprout stands of mountain hemlock and alpine fir. Crossing over the passes to the eastern side of the Cascades, you'll see how the wrung-out clouds leave this landscape to drought-tolerant species of lodgepole, western white pine, and ponderosa pine, surrounded by grassy meadows.

Highway 20, Washington's only paved road across this northern wilderness, was completed in 1972. The highway usually closes around Thanksgiving due to adverse weather conditions, opening again for the fishing season in April. Call Pass Reports at (900) 407–PASS for road condition information once the snowy season arrives around November 1. Late spring or early fall are the best times to avoid heavy traffic on the steep, narrow highway and to view colorful displays of spring flowers or autumn leaves. The **North Cascades National Park Office,** located at 2105 Highway 20 in Sedro Woolley, is a good place to stop for information as you approach from the west, or call (206) 865–5700. The office is open Saturday through Thursday from 8:00 A.M. to 4:30 P.M. and Fridays from 8:00 A.M. to 6:00 P.M.

The **North Cascades Institute,** also in Sedro Woolley, offers over seventy high-quality yearly seminars that delve into the magnificent natural, cultural, and aesthetic diversity of the Pacific

Northwest. The institute organizes small, informal classes taught by enthusiastic experts. Classes are held in natural settings. You can learn about butterflies, wildflowers, native carving, naturalist journals, wilderness poetry, photography, painting, archaeological sites, environmental ethics, and alpine ecology. Contact North Cascades Institute, 2105 Highway 20, Sedro Woolley 98284, or call (206) 856-5700.

Many visitors to northcentral Washington enjoy a full serving of excitement with a river rafting adventure. Over a dozen rivers are popular for rafting, ranging from a relaxing Class I to suicidal Class VI. Several professional rafting companies supply the equipment, information, and confidence beginners need to tackle a river. Most guided rafting trips concentrate on Class III and IV rivers; that is, rivers that have just enough rapids and white water to guarantee adventure and thrills. Some easy float trips are scheduled to observe eagles and osprey. For information call **Northwest Wilderness River Riders** at (206) 448-RAFT or **Alpine Whitewater** at (800) 926-RAFT.

Traveling east from Sedro Woolley, you'll follow the winding Skagit River, a designated National Wild and Scenic River, colored turquoise with glacial meltwaters. Take the turnoff north on Baker Lake Road if you wish to visit ⊃**Baker Lake,** a lovely mountain reservoir with campsites, trails, and lake access. You'll enjoy spectacular views of Mount Baker, due north, known to the local Nooksack tribe as Koma Kulshan, "the steep white mountain." **Shadow of the Sentinels,** on your right just past the Koma Kulshan Guard Station at Baker Lake's south end, is a pleasant half-mile, wheelchair-accessible trail and interpretive hike through old-growth forest. At **Rainbow Falls Viewpoint** (20 miles north of the highway on Baker Lake Road, then left on Forest Road 1130), you can see Rainbow Creek cascade down a 100-foot gorge, shattering sunlight into multicolored sprays. Several of the campsites along the lake are primitive and require visitors to bring water or purification equipment, while pump water is available at **Horseshoe Cove** and **Panorama Point campgrounds. Baker Lake Resort,** set between two bubbling creeks on the lake's north shore, has rustic lakefront cabins, forested or waterfront campsites, showers, boat rentals and launches, and the area's only store. Write P.O. Box 100, Concrete 98237, or call (206) 853-8325 for information and reservations.

⊃**Cascade Mountain Inn** is a pleasant mountain-view inn located south of the highway off Wild Road, 1 mile east of the Baker Lake turnoff at milepost 83. Well-traveled and hospitable innkeepers Ingrid and Gerhard Meyer have decorated each of their six rooms to reflect the best of the countries they've lived in, from the warm Peruvian room to the green tones and heather of Scotland. Guests enjoy hearty breakfasts, as well as good company around the fireplace in winter or around the campfire in summer. Contact the inn at 3840 Pioneer Lane, Concrete-Birdsview 98237 (800–826–0015 or 206–826–4333). Nearby **Shannon Lake,** the reservoir behind lower Baker Lake Dam, is the site of the largest nesting osprey colony in the state.

You'll see snow-capped peaks as you continue east on Highway 20. For a strenuous hike that leads to even more spectacular views, turn north off the highway at milepost 97 onto steep and winding Sauk Mountain Road. In 7 miles turn onto the first road to your right. In a quarter-mile this road ends at the trailhead to **Sauk Mountain Trail.** Three miles and 26 switchbacks later you'll have attained a panoramic view of the North Cascades, with vistas stretching back to Puget Sound and Mount Rainier on clear days. **Sauk Springs Trail,** just north of the highway at **Rockport State Park,** provides an easier hike on a barrier-free path. Five miles of trails surround the park's stand of Douglas fir trees, which are over 300 years old.

About 3 miles east on Highway 20, just past the town of Rockport, is the **Skagit River Bald Eagle Natural Area** with its viewpoints and interpretive signs overlooking the river. Designated sites such as this are the best places to watch eagles without disturbing them. The great birds flock here in autumn from as far away as Alaska to feast on chum salmon that are exhausted and dying after their incredible upstream trips from the sea.

At milepost 101 you'll find the ⊃**Cascadian Farm Organic Market,** a roadside stand that sells the Cascade Farm company's outstanding organically grown products. Cascade Farm organic foods are shipped all over the country. At this busy little stand you can taste delicious berry shortcakes, low-sodium pickles and sauerkraut, fresh salads, sweet corn, all-fruit sorbets, and espresso. There are shaded picnic tables and self-guided tours of the experimental gardens. The market is open June through mid-September from 10:00 A.M. to about 6:00 P.M. weekdays and to 9:00 P.M. on weekends. For more information or to order certified organic treats, contact Cascadian Farm at 5375 Highway 20, Rockport 98283, or call (206) 853–8629.

Near the confluence of the Skagit and Cascade rivers, the town of Marblemount has been the last-chance stop for food, fuel, and news for travelers heading into the high wilderness ever since miners trekked through these rugged mountains in the 1880s. **Mountain Song Restaurant** (206–873–2461) offers "bike food": natural, hearty meals especially appreciated by the many bicycle tourists who pedal on the North Cascades Highway each summer. The restaurant, featuring delicious homemade breads and desserts, is open daily from 8:00 A.M. to 9:00 P.M. The **Marblemount Ranger Station** has North Cascades National Park information and backcountry permits (206–873–4590).

Cascade River Road is a 25-mile gravel spur road heading southeast from Highway 20 at Marblemount, passing subalpine meadows on its way to the **Cascade Pass Trailhead.** This 3.7-mile trail leads to spectacular views of the North Cascades. As with all mountain trails, stick to the path to avoid damage to native vegetation or to yourself. Volunteers have carefully transplanted the area with fragile, high-elevation plants grown in Marblemount to help restore damage caused by overuse and abuse by careless visitors.

The Skagit River's aqua color deepens as it churns through billowing rapids in the increasingly narrow valley. Just west of the **Goodell Creek Campground,** you'll find the rough, winding gravel road that goes 4.7 miles to the **Thornton Lakes Trailhead.** From there, the steep 5-mile trail will reward you with exquisite views of alpine lakes with numerous mountains beyond.

The Skagit River Valley widens at **Newhalem,** a company town just off the highway. There you'll find picnic sites next to an old steam locomotive, a general store with souvenirs and supplies, gentle trails, and the ⊃**Seattle City Light Visitor Center.** The center has information about dam tours (mid-June through early September), which include scenic boat trips on Diablo Lake, rides 560 feet up the side of Sourdough Mountain on an antique incline railway (the last of its kind in the United States), and all-you-can-eat chicken dinners with homemade desserts at the Diablo Cookhouse. Call (206) 684–3030 for information and reservations.

At the end of Newhalem's Main Street you can stroll along the **Trail of the Cedars.** This self-guided loop nature trail, a third of a mile long, crosses a suspension bridge into the forest on the Skagit's south bank. **Ladder Creek Falls,** behind the Gorge Powerhouse, snakes its way through a beautiful landscaped garden of native plants and quiet pools, lit up at night with river-generated power. The open-grate bridge at the **Gorge Creek Scenic Lookout,** between mileposts 123 and 124 on Highway 20, provides breathtaking views of the 242-foot gorge below. The big parking lot makes this spot easily accessible to highway travelers.

To get farther from the crowds and your car, and thoroughly enjoy yourself in the process, we recommend a stay at the floating ⊃**Ross Lake Resort.** This unique isolated resort is not accessible by road; you must either hike on a 2-mile mountain trail from Highway 20 or enjoy a three-part journey that begins with a tugboat ride from the Ross Lake Resort parking lot on Diablo Lake at 8:30 A.M. or 3:00 P.M. Piles of food (visitors must bring their own since there is no store or restaurant at the resort), knapsacks, and people all jumble together in the small, bobbing tugboat as it chugs past rocky islands and into a narrow passageway between steep canyon walls. Near the foot of Ross Dam, resort staff (and occasionally a curious mule deer) meet travelers at the dock. With gear and people safely loaded onto open trucks, it's a short but bumpy ride up switchbacks through the forest and sparkling air to Ross Lake. Speedboats from the resort ferry guests across the lake to the cluster of comfortable wood cabins floating on huge cedar logs off the northwestern shore. When the wind picks up, the cabins gently sway, creating a pleasant creaking as the floats pull on their mooring lines. From your cabin's front stoop you can bask in the splendid water and mountain views and plan your day's adventure exploring Ross Lake.

The floating cabins were built in the 1930s as bunkhouses for loggers who harvested timber from the valley before it was flooded by Ross Dam. After this work was completed, the houseboats were converted into this rustic resort. Since the early 1980s they have been modernized with kitchens, plumbing, and electricity. Canoes and small motorboats are available for fishing or exploring the area's magnificent terrain. Hikers can arrange water-taxi service to trailheads for backcountry adventures. You can retrace the steps of writer Jack Kerouac, who watched for fires up-lake at **Desolation Peak** in 1956, or canoe deep into steep canyons such as **Devil's Creek** or **Ruby Arm.** The resort is open from mid-June through the end of October and gets especially busy when fishing

Ross Lake Resort

season starts in early July. For reservations, write to Ross Lake Resort, Rockport 98283, or call (206) 386–4437.

Back on Highway 20 heading east, you can stop for sweeping views of Diablo Lake and the hanging glaciers of Colonial and Pyramid peaks beyond from the overlook at milepost 131.8. A few miles farther, the **Happy Creek Forest Walk,** south of the highway, provides a barrier-free, boardwalk a third of a mile long past huge fallen and standing old-growth trees. Interpretive signs tell the forest's story to the sounds of the bubbling creek. Ross Lake stretches before you from the **Ross Lake Overlook,** north of the highway. There is trail access to the dam from here. A few miles farther east, at the **East Bank Trailhead,** a quarter-mile hike will take you to Ruby Creek, an important spawning area for native trout (no fishing allowed). In 3 miles on the trail, you can reach the shore of Ross Lake and in 28 miles, the Canadian border. **Canyon Creek Trailhead,** where Highway 20 veers southeast, marks the beginning of a short walk over a bridge to a turn-of-the-century mining site. About 2 miles up the trail, you'll see Rowley's Chasm, a 200-foot cleft in the rocky hillside.

The roadside scenery gets even more spectacular as you approach the passes. Creeks cascade down avalanche chutes— vertical alpine meadows of pillowy green velvet dotted with purple fireweed and red Indian paintbrush. There are several places to pull off the road to enjoy the views, such as the **Whistler Basin Overlook** at milepost 160, the barrier-free **Rainy Lake Trail,** or the point at which the 2,600-mile **Pacific Crest National Scenic Trail** from Mexico to Canada crosses the highway at Rainy Pass. Cast your gaze on the magnificence of Liberty Bell mountain, a jagged-edged precipice that looms above ↄ**Washington Pass Overlook** (milepost 162.2), a spectacular viewpoint perched 700 feet above the highway. The wheelchair-accessible loop path to the overlook offers close-up views of alpine plants and geology, from spiral-grained trees to smooth, glacier-carved stones. Located over a mile above sea level, Washington Pass is the North Cascades Highway's uppermost point. From here the highway hairpin-turns down a steep U-shaped valley into the drier terrain below Liberty Bell.

A semiarid landscape dominated by ponderosa pine surrounds you on the Cascade Mountains' eastern slopes as you descend into the **Methow Valley.** There are pleasant, streamside campgrounds along the way at **Klipchuck** and **Early Winters.** The latter also has a National Park Service Visitors Center and Ranger Station (509–996–2534) open daily, June 19 through Labor Day, from 10:00 A.M. to 4:00 P.M. The tiny village of **Mazama** is located a quarter-mile north of the highway at the upper end of the beautiful Methow Valley. At first glance, Mazama's quaint country store, gas station, and post office appear to be all that is left of this once-booming mining town. Look just beyond the village center to discover the ƆMazama **Country Inn,** a wonderful all-season retreat nestled in the forest between dry hills. Located at the edge of the **Pasayten Wilderness,** the inn's spacious wood lodge and comfortable rooms open onto miles of hiking, mountain bike, and well-groomed cross-country ski trails. The inn's cross-country ski rental shop offers tours and lessons by certified instructors. To relax after your wilderness adventures or from the urban grind you left behind, you can immerse yourself in the inn's outdoor hot tub overlooking the forest, or toast in the sauna. Hearty meals are served family style in winter and à la carte at the inn's restaurant in summer. The restaurant is open to travelers as to well as to overnight guests. During the winter when Highway 20 is closed, Mazama is accessible only from the southeast. Write to the Mazama Country Inn at P.O. Box 223, Mazama 98833, or call (509) 996–2681 from out of state or (800) 843–7951 within Washington.

There's lots to do in this area during the winter. **Rendezvous Outfitters** (P.O. Box 728, Winthrop 98862, 509–996–3287) offers backcountry hut-to-hut ski touring through the Okanogan National Forest for a combination of daytime adventure and overnight comfort. If you've ever wanted to experience the excitement of dogsledding, contact the **Malamute Express** (Route 2, Box 422, Twisp 98856; 509–997–6402). Roy and Sue Fuller will take you sledding through the pristine snowscapes of the Methow Valley, pulled by AKC-registered Alaskan malamutes, the "classic freighters" among sled dogs. The Fullers love their dogs and the sport, and they share this enthusiasm with their clients. If scenic horseback riding adventures are your style, consider a wilderness pack trip with **Early Winters Outfitting,** located nearby. Contact Aaron Lee or Judy Burkhart (P.O. Box 232, Mazama 98833; 509–996–2659 or 996–2681).

Mountain bicycling is also popular in the Methow Valley. For a glimpse of a gold miner's trials, mountain bikers ready for a challenge can undertake the treacherous 24-mile climb from Mazama to **Hart's Pass.** This road was created in 1900 as a 36-inch-wide wagon path to supply mines in the next valley and widened to its present width in 1935. The steep gravel road is still just one lane wide with turnouts. It skirts sheer glacier-carved cliffs, purple-red rocks full of rusted iron ore known as "red-beds," and giant layers of tilted stone; the twisted remnants of an ancient sea. The road divides at the pass. The east fork, the highest road in the state, follows the Pacific Crest Trail to Slate Peak, where a short footpath leads to an abandoned fire lookout with magnificent views. The rocky west fork plunges down along Slate Creek to the remains of Chancellor, an old mining town. For information on mountain bicycling in the Okanogan Forest, write to the Winthrop Ranger Office, P.O. Box 579, Winthrop 98862, or call (509) 996–2266. **Virginian Bike Rentals** (509–996–2535), on the east side of Winthrop, has plenty of mountain bikes and additional information on great local routes, from easy to hard-core.

Highway 20 traffic slows as it winds through **Winthrop,** a turn-of-the-century trading post now spruced up with a touristy Western theme. The crowded quaintness of the false-front stores, hotels, and restaurants is corny but fun, especially for children. The west side of town, beyond the highway, is a little more authentic, with historic buildings and a blacksmith shop that look more original than their facelifted counterparts in town. The **Schafer Museum,** in a historic log home on the hill one block above town, is worth a visit to glimpse some of the town's early history. The museum is open from 10:00 A.M. to 5:00 P.M. daily from Memorial Day to Labor Day. There are plenty of restaurants and lots of places to stay in the area, including simple motels, elegant bed and breakfasts, and rental cabins. For help finding a bed you can afford, call Central Reservations at (800) 422–3048 from within Washington or (509) 996–2148 from other states, Monday through Saturday from 9:00 A.M. to 6:00 P.M.

The **Eastside Winthrop-Twisp Road** is a pleasant, less-traveled route to the quiet, unpretentious town of Twisp. On the way, about 5 miles east of Winthrop, you can explore the world of firefighting at the **Cascades Smoke Jumpers Base** operated by the U.S. Forest Service. Contact the Twisp Ranger District (P.O. Box 188, Twisp 98856; 509–997–2131), Monday through Friday, 7:45 A.M. to 4:30 P.M., for tour information. The ranger station also has a wealth of suggestions for backcountry hikes in the Twisp River Valley region.

A couple miles past Twisp, the highway forks. Highway 20 continues east to Okanogan. Highway 153 follows the Methow River as it winds and glistens over its pebbly bed southeast to Pateros. On this route, you'll pass the pleasant community of Methow, then plunge into orchard country as the river gorge deepens before its confluence with the Columbia River. A few miles west of Pateros, you can enjoy a delightful retreat at ↄ**Amy's Manor.** This stately hillside house, built in 1928, offers beautiful views of the river valley and great hospitality, thanks to hosts Barb and Rodney Nickell. Guests can wander through the estate's 170 acres to view wildlife and farm animals, enjoy fishing, and even play tennis on a private court. For information write Amy's Manor, P.O. Box 411, Pateros 98846, or call (509) 923–2334.

Okanogan Valley

The Okanogan Valley stretches from the British Columbia border at Oroville south to the Columbia River. Much of the land along the river is planted with fruit orchards. The land above the river valley is drier, covered with rolling grass and sagebrush meadows dotted with occasional stands of ponderosa pine, glacially deposited boulders, and lakes. Okanogan is the Kalispel word for rendezvous or "gathering place." For the many bands who traded and held potlatches here, and later for the hordes of miners and settlers who displaced them, this fertile valley has been and continues to be a center for human activity and celebration.

Highway 20 merges with Highway 97 in the city of Okanogan. Be sure to visit the ↄ**Okanogan County Historical Museum,** located on the Highway 97 business alternate between Okanogan and Omak, open daily from 11:00 A.M. to 5:00 P.M. Lovingly created displays cover local geography and history and include descriptions of Indian and pioneer life. Outside is a collection of log buildings, with stores, a settlers' cabin, a blacksmith's shop, and a saloon. The **Bread Line** cafe, a few miles north in Omak, offers good food and live entertainment, often featuring well-known performers when they travel through the area.

ↄ**Conconully** was once a rough pioneer and mining community that has become a favorite all-season fishing resort (featuring ice fishing in winter), located high in the pine-covered hills. To

get there take Conconully Road north from Okanogan, or Riverside Cutoff Road west from Riverside. It's a 22-mile trip over
sagebrush-covered hills, past small ranches and the Pioneer Rest
Cemetery. Conconully is a busy little town, home to a few small
resorts, two stores, and the annual Gene Curtis Memorial 25 Mile
Mule Race. Conconully State Park has a public beach as well as
camping and picnicking sites.

To visit the site of ⊃**Ruby City,** the "Queen City of Okanogan
County" during the late nineteenth century, follow Conconully
Road 3 miles east of Conconully, then turn south on Salmon
Creek Road, a gravel road. In about 3 miles, after crossing a
creek, you'll see a marker describing Ruby's short but exciting
history. Founded during the silver boom of 1886, its Main Street
of stores, saloons, and land offices once stretched for a quarter-
mile. The town was abandoned in 1893 when nearby silver
mines, such as the First Thought, Arlington, and Fourth of July,
gave out. Since then the forest has overgrown the site. Now,
except for a historical society plaque, there is little indication of
the excitement, wealth, and disappointment that occurred there
so many years ago. You can continue on Salmon Creek Road to
the town of Okanogan if you don't mind driving another 7
miles on good gravel.

Whether you want a good meal or a fun place to stay, local
folks recommend the **Hidden Hills Guest Ranch** (144 Fish
Lake Road, Tonasket 98855; 800–468–1890 or 509–486–1890), a
re-created Western inn that promises "an 1890s experience with
1990s convenience." The restaurant features hearty breakfasts
and family-style dinners with a menu that changes daily as the
market and cook Martha Thomas dictate. The ranch makes an
ideal retreat for families. To get there, turn west from Highway 20
on Pine Creek Road 5 miles north of Riverside. Watch for the
ranch on your right in 6 miles, after Pine Creek Road becomes
Fish Lake Road.

⊃**Orchard Country Inn** (First and Antwine, P.O. Box 634,
Tonasket 98855; 509–486–1923) is easy to miss if you never stray
from Tonasket's main drag. Located in a quiet hillside neighborhood, this friendly home is well known to bicyclists traveling on
the popular Northern Tier bicycle route charted by the Bikecentennial organization. The inn's basement is devoted to Youth
Hostel accommodations, with eighteen beds, two bathrooms, a
big kitchen, and a comfortable common area where international

travelers socialize. The upstairs has been tastefully renovated to suit the home's original 1920s style, with beautiful valley views and peaceful ambience. Bed and breakfast guests wake to fresh coffee at their door, and delicious home-baked treats are provided at the breakfast table of innkeepers Joy and John Barnhart.

East of Tonasket on Highway 20, the tiny community of **Wauconda** offers a great introduction to the open beauty of the Okanogan Highlands. You'll pass a scattered collection of homes, old homestead cabins, and barns set in an expansive 3,000-foot plateau. The ⊃**Wauconda Store and Cafe** (509–486–4010), a one-stop store-gas station-cafe-sawshop-gallery-meeting place just south of the highway, is worth a stop. Dean and Cindy Dyer's warm, wood-paneled cafe decorated with local art and historical photos offers great views of the rolling valley and serves delicious pies and other home-baked treats.

The ⊃**Bonaparte Lake Resort** (509–486–2828) has cabins (with kitchens but no bedding), camping, gas, and a lodge with a small store and cafe famous for its great hamburgers. To get there, turn north about 3 miles west of Wauconda off Highway 20 onto a 6-mile country road that winds along Bonaparte Creek through meadows and forests. The National Forest also has several campgrounds in the area. **Lost Lake Campground** to the north (turn left off Bonaparte Creek Road onto Myers Creek Road) has several fine hiking trails, including the easy Big Tree Trail to see 600-year-old western larches, and the Strawberry Mountain Trail offering magnificent views from hillsides covered with wild strawberries. Write to the Tonasket District Ranger, P.O. Box 466, Tonasket 98855, or call (509) 486–2186, for more information.

Take your time on the corrugated road north from Lost Lake to **Chesaw.** Asian placer miner Chee Saw and his native wife, Julia Lumm, didn't know when they settled down to farm on Myers Creek that their stream crossing would become the sight of a spirited turn-of-the-century boomtown for miners and homesteaders flooding the Colville Reservation when it opened for mining and settlement. You'll find the town has reverted to a sleepier demeanor, with a string of small buildings and hillside homes scattered along the road.

You can learn about a new "micro" gold rush using chemical extraction methods that threatens to shatter the area's peace and water quality from the **Okanogan Highlands Alliance,** c/o Columbiana Publishing, Chesaw Route, Box 83-F, Oroville 98844

(509–485–3844). Rick Gillespie and his family welcome visitors interested in local environmental issues to visit their publishing center in Chesaw. The **Country Gift Shop** up the road features a colorful collection of handmade treasures by more than thirty rural artisans, as well as antique quilts and collectibles. Carol Hull's cottage is open in summer from 10:00 A.M. to 5:00 P.M. and in winter until 4:00 P.M. Thursday through Monday (509–485–2100).

Watch for the **Hee Hee Stone** monument on a hillside to your right as you head west to Molson and Oroville. Once the site of a native trail, the great rock that marked this magical spot where a legendary Spokane woman turned to stone was blown to bits by drunken prospectors in 1905. The road winds 5 miles through dry hills past mullein, bunchgrass, and lupine to the turnoff north (right) for 5 miles over wide rolling fields to Molson. This rugged highland town of twenty residents boomed with the arrival of the railway in 1906 and busted thirty years later when the railway moved south.

Molson's two historical museums are worth seeing. The ⊃Molson School, open daily from 10:00 A.M. to 5:00 P.M. Memorial Day weekend through Labor Day, offers three floors of well-organized displays highlighting local history. After browsing through the classrooms and library upstairs, the vintage clothing and furniture on the main floor, or the huge tool collection downstairs, you can enjoy homemade treats and lemonade provided by museum volunteers in a breezy main-floor classroom. The **Old Molson Outdoor Museum,** open during daylight hours for self-guided tours from April through December, exudes an Old West feeling with its nineteenth-century cabins, shingle mill, mining and farm tools, and storefronts. Both museums are free, but donations are requested. **Sidley** and **Molson lakes** just north of town are popular with travelers who like to fish. Birdwatchers also delight in the array of waterfowl, from blue-billed ruddy ducks to long-necked canvasbacks, feeding amidst reeds and islands in the tiny lakes.

You can continue past the lakes to Oroville-Taroda Creek Road on scenic but primitive Nine Mile Road, which skirts the Canadian border, or retrace your path through Molson. Oroville-Taroda Creek Road descends through steep, rocky slopes into pine forests and rangelands scattered with old wood barns before it re-emerges among the green orchards of the Okanogan River

Old Molson Outdoor Museum

Valley. At Oroville, zigzag left onto Emry, then right onto Cherry Street, then left onto Central Avenue to Main Street.

Oro, the Spanish word for gold, bespeaks this town's early history as a miner's mecca. Oroville's original Great Northern Depot has been restored as a museum and community hall on the corner of Twelfth and Ironwood streets, one block west of Main Street. The **Oroville Depot,** open Tuesdays and Thursdays from 1:00 to 4:00 P.M., provides insight into the town's history as a railroad, mining, and agricultural center buffeted by changing times. One change that is certainly for the better is the town's increasing cultural and commercial diversity. **Cricko's Restaurant** in downtown Oroville (1321 Main Street; 509–476–2037) offers light and tasty meals from central Mexico. Cricko's is open daily from 11:30 A.M. to 9:00 P.M.

For a look at a real railroad ghost town, follow signs west on Central Avenue to ⊃**Nighthawk.** This winding road hugs the northern shore of the beautiful Similkameen River. There are plenty of places to pull over and absorb the valley's rugged beauty. Watch for eagles in the tall cottonwoods that grace the Similkameen River before the road forks south. You can see Nighthawk nestled in the valley to your left, strung along the abandoned railway line in quiet testimony to what once was a bustling railroad town. You'll get a brief close-up glimpse of the old town interspersed with current farmhouses after you cross the bridge into the town. The rough wood remains of the Kaaba-Texas Mill, surrounded by gold-colored tailings, lies across the Similkameen River to your right. These sites are now private and best appreciated from a distance. There is also a trail on the abandoned railroad right of way connecting Nighthawk with Oroville which local people often use for mountain bike rides. For information about local attractions, write to the Oroville Tourist Information Center at P.O. Box 536, Oroville 98844, or call (509) 476–2739.

The road south from Nighthawk hugs the hillside across from the steep talus slopes of the Cascade foothills. You'll pass a public fishing spot on the creek north of bowl-shaped Palmer Lake. **Chopaka Lodge** (1913 Loomis Highway, Loomis 98827; 509–223–3131) at the lake's north end is a lovely spot with three log cabins on a bluff overlooking the water, surrounded by fruit trees. Follow the lakeshore southeast past hillside orchards and lakeside cabins and homes. ⊃**Split Rock Park** at the lake's south end makes a great stop for a picnic on a sandy beach surrounded by delicate willows, punctuated by a big piece of rock cut sharply in two. The park is maintained by local residents (you can help by bringing out your own trash) who flock here to swim, boat, or play from the shallow south shore.

Continue southwest to **Loomis,** traversing dry hillsides above the green Sinlahekin Valley. Loomis is another quiet town that boomed during the gold rush of the 1890s and busted soon after. You'd never know from the orchards, old houses, and one-block main street that this was once the largest city in the county. South from Loomis you can take a primitive but beautiful road through the **Sinlahekin Valley and Wildlife Area** back to Conconully.

East from Loomis on the Loomis-Oroville Road is narrow Spectacle Lake, rimmed with cattails, dry hills, and remnants of an old wooden irrigation flume. There are several rustic resorts along this roadside lake but the best one is hidden away to the north on secluded Wannacut Lake. Watch for the sign on your left past Spectacle Lake for ⊃**Sun Cove Resort and Guest Ranch,** an idyllic family retreat on the shores of a clear, cold mineral lake. The road winds dramatically up out of the green valley laced with irrigation canals onto 3 miles of gravel. You can also get there directly from Oroville on a 10-mile, mainly gravel road by following signs on Twelfth Avenue west of the Oroville Depot. The gravel routes there may be rough, but are worth the trip. The fully equipped log cabins and larger cottages (available by the week without bedding) are comfortable and charming with beautiful lake views. Besides excellent fishing opportunities, the wooded grounds provide plenty of fun activities for both children and adults, including hiking trails, a swimming pool, playground, and sports equipment. The Bear's Den (the resort office and meeting area) offers snacks, groceries, and reading and laundry facilities. The resort is open from April through November. Contact Sun Cove Resort, Route 2, Box 1294, Oroville 98844, or call (509) 476–2223.

If you don't take the turnoff to Sun Cove, you can continue straight on the Loomis-Oroville Road past Whitestone Lake and merge right onto the Tonasket-Oroville Westside Road. This lesstraveled route traverses the hills west of the Okanogan River, parallel to Highway 97. During summer, keep an eye out for fresh-fruit stands along the way to delight your taste buds. You can cross the river to Highway 97 at Tonasket or continue south until the highways merge at the north end of Wagonroad Coulee.

Stehekin

⊃**Stehekin** is nestled in a spectacular wooded valley at the western end of Lake Chelan. This charming community with fewer than 100 full-time residents is accessible only by traveling along the 60-mile-length of Lake Chelan, and it isn't on the way to anywhere except hundreds of square miles of wilderness. Despite its isolation, Stehekin is generous to tourists, offering a museum, stores, restaurant, bakery, bike rental, and resorts. But we're not talking big. Each of these services is small, simple, and friendly.

Two ferries sail daily between Chelan and Stehekin. The elegant old *Lady of the Lake* takes four hours to travel each way. The *Lady Express* does the same trip in a little over two hours. We highly recommend the slower trip, which provides enough time to enjoy the surrounding splendor. To make the trip extra interesting, Forest Service rangers offer presentations on local natural history during the boat trip to help visitors better understand the forest environment. For schedules, write to the Lake Chelan Boat Company at P.O. 186, Chelan 98816, or call (509) 682–2224.

Stehekin is the starting point for many wilderness expeditions, so you are likely to share the ferry with at least a few heavily loaded adventurers who will soon be off for extended trips into surrounding mountains. The boat may stop anywhere along the shore for passengers headed into the woods. Up the valley from Stehekin are several wilderness camps accessible by foot or shuttle bus service. The Pacific Crest Trail, which meanders from British Columbia to Mexico, is one of the many breathtaking hikes that pass through the Stehekin Valley. If you're interested in camping and hiking, you'll need to stop in at the **Golden West Lodge Information Center,** up the hill from the boat dock in Stehekin, for backcountry travel advice and permits. The center is open daily from 8:00 A.M. to 4:30 P.M. from mid-June through mid-September.

For a gentler adventure, with plenty of outdoor flavor, we recommend the **Stehekin Valley Ranch** (P.O. Box 38, Stehekin 98852; 509–682–4677), which is open from mid-June to the last week of September. Set amidst maple trees on the edge of an alfalfa field, 9 miles up the Stehekin Valley, this quiet guest ranch offers hearty meals with pleasant accommodations rustic enough to satisfy outdoor enthusiasts but civilized enough to include hot showers. The ranch arranges package trips that include either boat or floatplane trips to Stehekin, rafting on the swift Stehekin River, and horseback rides to a beautiful mountain lake on gentle, trail-wise horses, as well as meals and lodging. Guests can arrange drop-off and pickup services to and from the many spectacular hikes in the area.

In Stehekin you can go mountain-biking (**Discovery Bikes** located at the boat landing rents bikes by the hour or day), ride on the National Park Service's shuttle bus, or enjoy the easy 3.5-mile hike up the valley to view **Rainbow Falls.** Just a short walk from the main road puts you directly at the base of 312 feet of cascading water that will cool and delight you with its rainbow mist. For a taste of history, you can explore the old one-room Stehekin School down the road from the falls or walk on the delightful pathway along a mossy irrigation canal to the Buckner orchard and homestead. For sustenance on your return trip, stop at the **Stehekin Pastry Company** for delicious, fresh-baked treats (open May 15 through October 15).

Wenatchee Valley

The Columbia River is tamed in the center of the state by the Rocky Reach, Rock Island, Wanapum, and Priest Rapids dams, which create long, narrow reservoirs, generate electricity, and provide irrigation for this extremely fertile region. Like the Okanogan Valley to the north, nearly all available plots of land along the Columbia River and several smaller valleys to the west are planted in orchards, making this one of the nation's prime sources of apples and other fruit. These valleys also offer many recreation activities. Boating, swimming, fishing, and bicycling are popular during the long, sunny summers; skiing and ice-skating are popular in winter.

The town of **Chelan,** set on the southeast shore of its namesake lake, is a popular tourist destination. It's a pleasant, clean town with plenty of attractions, including lake beaches and a local historical museum. Visit the beautiful 4-mile-long Chelan River Gorge through which the churning river drops 405 feet to the Columbia River. Downtown Chelan is a pleasant place for strolling, shopping, and leisurely eating. You'll find a wide selection of accommodations, including **Mary Kay's Whaley Mansion Inn** (415 Third Avenue, Chelan 98816; 800–729–2408 or 509–682–5735) and the **Brick House Inn** (304 Wapato Avenue, Chelan 98816; 509–682–4791). Both offer excellent accommodations in the downtown area. Situated on a hill just above the town is the 1904 **Highland Guest House** (121 East Highland Avenue, Chelan 98816; 509–682–2892).

If you head east on Highway 2 from the Columbia River, about 25 miles south of Chelan (via Highway 151), you'll climb through wheat-covered rolling hills to the town of Waterville. The ⊃**Douglas County Historical Museum** on Highway 2 on the west side of town has interesting displays, including an extensive rock collection. Ask the museum docent to turn off the fluorescent lights so you can view the gem collection under ultraviolet illumination. In front of the museum is one of the large metal buckets that was once part of an overhead conveyer system that, at the turn of the century, carried wheat 2,400 feet down to the river where it could be loaded on ships. Waterville is a pleasant community with many old houses and a beautiful county courthouse. The **Tower House** bed and breakfast (305 West Ash, Waterville 98858; 509–745–8320), a fine old house lovingly restored by hosts Fred and Phyllis Rigg, is a welcome place to stay in town. Guests have a choice of two upstairs rooms and enjoy a delightful gourmet breakfast.

Mountain Passes, Valleys, and Canyons

Highway 2 goes west from Wenatchee, through the Bavarian tourist theme-town of Leavenworth, through the beautiful Wenatchee National Forest, over Stevens Pass, and down into the Puget Sound area. For an enjoyable side trip, turn north on Highway 209 at Leavenworth. This takes you up Chumstick Creek Canyon and through the village of Plain. Turn left in Plain to return to Highway 2, or turn right to Lake Wenatchee where you can stop at the lakeside **Cougar Inn.** Hosts Tom and Dodee Olson offer an elegant but informal restaurant, open for breakfast, lunch, and dinner, and plenty of vacation activities for guests. You can rent a boat for fishing and exploring the lake, or cross-country skis in winter, and at night the inn offers spectacular views from the Moonshine cocktail room. For information write to the Cougar Inn, 23379 Highway 207, Leavenworth 98826, or call (509) 763–3354.

The trip up to **Stevens Pass** is spectacular, but not nearly as dramatic as it must have been for travelers in the late nineteenth century when the first railroad line crossed the Cascade Mountains here. The original route included 13 miles of switchbacks cut into the mountainside that required the train to stop on spur tracks, change the track switch, then reverse up the next leg. It was slow and precarious, greatly limiting the weight and speed of the trains. In 1900 a 2½-mile tunnel was completed under the pass that eliminated most of this climb. Electric-powered engines were used in the tunnel because regular coal-fired steam engines left passengers suffocating. But the approach to the tunnel still required trains to pass under steep mountain cliffs, and after snowslides caused a train accident that killed 96 people in 1910, the 8-mile Cascade Tunnel, currently the longest railroad tunnel in use in North America, was constructed.

You can still see remnants of the railroad camps along the highway at Wellington (north of the highway at milepost 61), the west portal of the older tunnel where the 1910 train accident occurred, and at Berne (at milepost 72), where workers lived while constructing the newer tunnel. A cooperative effort between the Burlington Northern railroad, the Mount Baker-Snoqualmie National Forest, and private organizations is under way to convert the abandoned railroad grade to the older, 2½-mile tunnel into the **Iron Goat Trail,** which will allow the public access to the abandoned tunnel's entrance and perhaps eventually allow hikers, bicyclists, and equestrians to go right through the mountains. For information on the status of this project, write to the Skykomish Ranger District office at P.O. Box 305, Skykomish 98288, or call (206) 677–2414.

Highway 97 crosses the Wenatchee National Forest between Wenatchee and Ellensburg. The current route over Swauk Pass is beautiful enough, but for a special treat take the old highway over spectacular **Blewett Pass,** if you don't mind a narrow, winding, poorly maintained road. Watch for the turnoff to Blewett Pass Road. Except for occasional logging trucks, you're likely to have the road to yourself. It's also a popular route with bicyclists. For a tamer adventure take Liberty Road 2 miles east from Highway 97 to the town of ⊃**Liberty,** the oldest mining town site in Washington state. Originally established as Williams in 1880, then renamed Meaghersville in 1897, it finally became Liberty in 1912 when the post office was moved from another community of that name. It's a secluded, one-street town consisting of a couple dozen modest homes, many of them log cabins, and the Liberty Gift Shop, where you can enjoy ice cream or a hot drink, depending on the season.

Kittitas County

The Kittitas Valley pushes into the eastern slope of the Cascade Mountains in the center of Washington state, surrounded on three sides by forests and towering peaks. Railroad buffs will enjoy a pilgrimage to South Cle Elum for the accommodations of ⊃**The Moore House Bed and Breakfast Inn** (526 Marie Street, P.O. Box 629, South Cle Elum 98943; 800–2–2–TWAIN or 509–674–5939). The Moore consists of a railroad workers' bunkhouse now converted into private rooms, and two comfortable cabooses, which can accommodate up to five guests each. The buildings are filled with railroad memorabilia, including tools, switch lights, toy trains, and conductors' uniforms. Innkeepers Eric and Cindy Sherwood provide delicious breakfasts in a bright dining room decorated with railroad lanterns and model trains. According to Eric, old-timers still drop in occasionally to see the rooms where they stayed between runs and tell stories as only old-time railroad men can.

Families will appreciate the inn's play equipment and rooms with bunk beds available for children. **Iron Horse Trail State Park,** a 25-mile nonmotorized portion of the John Wayne Trail system, runs adjacent to the inn, making it an ideal overnight spot for trail users. In summer, covered wagons follow the trail through the Yakima River Canyon and back to the inn for a tasty outdoor barbecue. Paddock facilities for horse-riding guests can be found in the inn's back yard. Visitors can rent mountain bikes, enjoy pleasant riverside walks, or try cross-country skiing, all within easy reach of the inn's front door. In the winter the inn is also a favorite stop for sleigh riders.

Downtown Ellensburg has a historic district that is ideal for strolling. Contact the Ellensberg Chamber of Commerce (436 North Sprague Street, 98926; 509–925–3137) for a walking-tour guide. Along the way you'll discover over two dozen ornate brick buildings constructed between the 1880s and 1910, most of which have been renovated and are used by small businesses from bakeries to sports stores. The **Clymer Museum and Gallery,** in the 1901 Ramsey Building at 416 North Pearl, highlights Western art, especially the work of local historical painter John Clymer, who captured details of life in Western America. The museum exhibits a variety of contemporary regional artists. You'll also see public art along the streets of Ellensburg, including the life-size Ellensburg bull sculpture relaxing on a downtown bench and the ready-to-shoot cowboy sculpture guarding the corner of Fifth and Pearl. A few blocks farther, at 101 Pearl, is **Dick & Jane's Spot,** a house displaying dynamic artwork made from bicycle wheels, mirrors, and reflectors, called "art for the heart, from the heart."

Ellensburg has cowboy roots that are proudly displayed at the annual National Western Art Show & Auction (held the third weekend in May) and the Ellensburg Rodeo and County Fair (held Labor Day weekend). A horse-drawn trolley that travels between downtown and the Central Washington University campus invokes the community's history and offers a fun way to see the city. The same company offers limousine service in smaller horse-drawn wagons for special events. Contact **Ellensburg Equine Trolley, Ltd.** at (509) 962–1889 for schedule and reservation information.

◯**Murphy's Country Bed and Breakfast** is a charming place to stay near Ellensburg. Hostess Doris Murphy carefully maintains her beautiful turn-of-the-century country home for others to enjoy. The large porch constructed of local stone and shaded by large maple and pine trees offers visitors a cool and quiet spot to relax and enjoy the bucolic view. The house includes the best of antique elegance and modern comforts. Doris Murphy's professional baking experience guarantees that visitors will enjoy the home-cooked farm breakfast. Guests' horses are welcome to stay in a secure pasture and corral for a small additional charge. For information write Murphy's Bed and Breakfast, Route 1, Box 400, Ellensburg 98926, or call (509) 925–7986.

The old road between Ellensburg and Yakima, Highway 821, follows the beautiful ◯**Lower Yakima River Canyon** for approximately 25 miles. It's a favorite route for sightseeing, due to beautiful views of the river and the Cascade foothills, and for bicycling, due to the relatively light traffic. Hunting, fishing, and bird-watching are popular in the area. Because this stretch of the river is relatively slow and safe, it's also a haven for beginning rafters and kayakers. The main rafting season is from mid-April through October. River Raft Rentals (Route 4, Box 275, Ellensburg 98926; 509–964–2145) can provide two-person inflatable kayaks, three- and eight-person rafts, safety equipment, instruction, and delivery. Special services, including catered gourmet meals, are also available. The canyon is administered by the U.S. Bureau of Land Management, which maintains rest stops, a boat launch, and a footbridge to allow hikers and equestrians to cross the river to its undeveloped side. For information contact the BLN Wenatchee Area Office at 1133 North Western Avenue, Wenatchee 98801, or call (509) 662–4223.

The **Vantage Highway** from Ellensburg to the Columbia River is a wonderful route east that misses the traffic of Interstate 90 and offers views of rich farmlands that give way to rolling sagebrush meadows. The highway passes by the **Quilomene Wildlife Area,** a 45,000-acre preserve popular with hunters. Watch for ⊃**Gingko Petrified Forest State Park** to your left as you descend to the Columbia River. The park has two short trails through sagebrush environs highlighting exposed "trees of stone." This area is rich with wildlife, including mammals, reptiles, and birds that have learned to live in the relatively dry sagebrush landscape. Fifteen to twenty million years ago this land was moist and lush, covered with swamps and thick forests. When layers of lava covered the area, many logs that had sunk to the bottom of shallow lakes were entombed and eventually became petrified after minerals replaced organic materials. Over 200 species of trees have been identified among the many outstanding examples of petrified wood; many are extinct, but a few, including the gingko tree, have changed little from their ancestors. Brochures at the trailhead will help you identify the ancient gingko, spruce, and fir logs scattered along the path. **The Gingko Petrified Forest Interpretive Center** (509–856–2700) in Vantage, open from 10:00 A.M. to 6:00 P.M. daily from mid-May through mid-September, is well worth a visit.

The highway ends at Vantage, where you'll cross the wide Columbia River. We recommend that you take the 5-mile detour south on Highway 243 to the ⊃**Wanapum Dam Visitors Center,** open April through October, where you can tour the dam facilities and visit a museum describing the area's history. The museum offers a detailed description of the native people who inhabited the region for thousands of years and a surprisingly frank portrayal of the impacts of white culture on this tribe. The Wanapum, whose name means "river people," had a rich culture based on fishing the Chiawana (Columbia River) using a variety of tools and techniques perfected over centuries. They had deep religious beliefs and a desire to live peacefully and in their own way. Unfortunately, their traditional homeland along the Columbia River placed the Wanapums in the middle of waves of Europeans who arrived over the past century. The tribe was not recognized by early treaties, but despite many difficulties, tribal members struggled peacefully for decades to maintain their community and preserve their dignity during conflicts with settlers. Although the dam itself flooded the tribe's historic village site and ended the traditional livelihood of salmon fishing, the Wanapum people have continued to exist and are working to create a viable future for their community. The museum also describes the steamboats that plied the river in earlier days and the history of homesteading on the Columbia Plateau.

Off the Beaten Path in Southcentral Washington

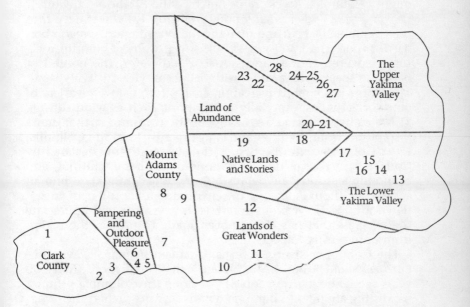

1. Cedar Creek Grist Mill
2. Beacon Rock State Park
3. Bonneville Dam
4. Columbia Gorge Interpretive Center
5. Carson Hot Mineral Springs Resort
6. Wind River Nursery and Arboretum
7. Peaceful Pastures Llama Ranch Bed and Breakfast
8. Trout Lake Country Inn
9. Conboy Lake National Wildlife Refuge
10. She-Who-Watches
11. Maryhill Museum
12. Goldendale Observatory State Park
13. Chukar Cherry Company
14. Dykstra House Restaurant
15. Le Ma Cuisine
16. Yakima Valley Cheese Company
17. Granger Berry Patch Farm
18. Yakima Nation Cultural Heritage Center
19. Fort Simcoe State Park Heritage Site
20. Zillah
21. El Ranchito
22. Central Washington Agricultural Museum
23. Ahtanum Mission
24. Yakima Greenway
25. Yakima Interurban Trolley Line
26. Birchfield Manor Restaurant and Bed and Breakfast
27. Desert Rose
28. Indian Painted Rocks

Southcentral Washington

Two geographic features dominate southcentral Washington: the lower Columbia River Gorge and the Yakima Valley. The mighty Columbia River drains much of the Pacific Northwest. It is over a mile wide at many points, cutting 1,000 feet deep into the Columbia Plateau and marking the Washington–Oregon border for more than 300 miles. With steep walls of colorful rock, forest-covered shores, and sun-sparkled water, the gorge is a region of spectacular beauty, with delightful views at every bend. The Gorge is a famous recreation area, offering a wide variety of outdoor activities, especially water sports such as wind surfing. This area has attracted a growing artistic community that draws inspiration from the dramatic landscape. In 1986 the Columbia River Gorge became the first National Scenic Area declared by Congress, in recognition of its unique aesthetic, cultural, and economic features. The details of how to accommodate human activities without damaging the environment are still being negotiated among the various interests, but visitors will appreciate the progress that has already been made to protect the region from unnecessary impacts.

The Columbia River Gorge has changed in many ways since European and American explorers first visited more than 200 years ago. Then, native people lived along the Columbia's shores, harvesting abundant salmon and native plants such as the camas flower root. Over time, white settlers established farms and a logging industry; dammed the rivers, which destroyed aboriginal fishing sites; and built towns. Interstate 84 on Oregon's side of the river attracts most through traffic, leaving Highway 14 to wind leisurely along Washington's north shore for use by local residents and adventurous tourists. Driving or bicycling along this route, you'll enjoy seeing the towering landscape, watching an endless parade of river traffic, and visiting friendly communities strung like beads on a necklace.

In contrast, the Yakima Valley is known for its agriculture, especially fruit orchards and vineyards. The valley is a virtual Garden of Eden filled with orchards and vegetable fields. Its rich volcanic soil, abundant summer sun, and irrigation from nearby mountains makes this one of the most productive agricultural regions in the world. During spring you can see the blocks of trees erupt into a colorful patchwork of blossoms. In summer, cherries, apples, pears, plums, apricots, and peaches hang ripening under brilliant hot sun. A progression of crops is harvested from early summer (cherries) through autumn (late apples), offering continually changing sights and tastes.

Apples are the valley's largest crop. You can spot the older orchards by their various-size trees and numerous varieties, including red Delicious, Pippins, Granny Smiths, golden Delicious, and some you may never have heard of, such as Winter Banana. Most newer orchards have one primary variety, either red Delicious or Granny Smith, with a different variety planted every tenth row for pollination, since most apple varieties won't pollinate themselves. Newer orchards are often planted with dwarf trees that are easy to irrigate and pick. The Yakima Valley also brims with pear, peach, and cherry orchards, vegetable farms, hop fields, and vineyards. The hop vines are grown on elaborate cable structures strung on poles ten to fifteen feet in the air. Decades ago hops were hand-harvested, which attracted hundreds of temporary workers, many of whom were Native Americans. Old-timers still recall music, dancing, and fun lasting late into the warm autumn nights during harvesting at the hop-worker camps.

In recent years a respected wine industry has developed in the Yakima Valley. The valley boasts a climate and soil conditions similar to the Bordeaux and Burgundy regions of France. Within the valley you can visit more than a dozen wineries, ranging from small, family-run operations, such as the Bonair Winery (described as a "little hobby that got out of hand"), to major labels such as Chateau Ste. Michelle. Even people who don't drink wine can enjoy touring a winery to learn about the wine-making process and to picnic on the grounds. Visitors can obtain information from the Yakima Valley Wine Growers Association by writing to P.O. Box 39, Grandview 98930, or by picking up one of its brochures at a Yakima area winery or tourist information office. You can also get a listing of specialty farms (many of which offer U-pick) from the Yakima Valley Direct Marketing Association by sending a self-addressed stamped envelope to Farm Products Map, 1731 Beam Road, Granger 98932. This information is also distributed at many Yakima Valley businesses.

The Yakima Valley is culturally diverse. A large Spanish-speaking population supplies much of the labor. Many farms and small businesses in the Yakima area are owned or managed by Latinos, including several Mexican restaurants. The Yakima Indian Reservation covers a major part of the lower valley, encompassing the towns of Wapato and Toppenish, and the new tribal center and museum. You'll find opportunities to learn about traditional and contemporary native culture, including a magnificent tribal center with museum, craft shop, and restaurant. You can also learn about pioneer life and traditional farming activities at local history museums in many Yakima Valley communities.

The Yakima River, which meanders down the valley is a braided river, which means that it regularly changes its course, much to the frustration of engineers who tried to control it in the past. Now much of the riverbed is a natural wetland preserve, with lovely places to view wildlife and enjoy quiet away from the rest of the valley's bustle. Fishing, hunting, bird-watching, and bicycling are all popular activities in the Yakima Valley area. Interstate 82 goes down the center of the Yakima Valley, carrying most through traffic. We recommend that you travel on the Valley's numerous lesser-traveled highways and local roads to enjoy a closer view of valley life. Washington's southcentral region also includes the dry landscape of the Horse Haven Hills, the desert around the Tri-Cities, and the forested peaks of the southern Cascade Mountains.

Clark County

The ⊃**Cedar Creek Grist Mill,** built in 1876, is the oldest active industrial facility in Washington. It's a beautiful old building in an idyllic location on the steep, forested slope above the rushing creek, unchanged for over a hundred years. Although rough-hewn and unpretentious, the mill was for generations the center of local industry and social activities, the site of dances, parties, and musical shows. The mill is now a working museum, with a water-powered stone flour mill and machine shop and an upstairs museum with photos and artifacts from the mill's history.

Neglected for decades, this historic building and its milling machinery has been carefully rebuilt since 1980 thanks to volunteer efforts coordinated by the Friends of the Cedar Creek Grist Mill. Much of this reconstruction is done by work parties using traditional tools and techniques, including broadaxes and

adzes to form the massive replacement beams used in the renovation. Now, as a century ago, water from Cedar Creek is diverted
through a wood flume to the mill building, down the penstock (a
vertical pipe made of wood like an old barrel), driving a Leffel tur-
bine, which powers a shaft, which runs a leather drive belt,
which turns the millstones, which grinds wheat into flour. An
additional drive belt powers a machine shop and a small genera-
tor for lighting. When it is operating, the mill is like a busy and
noisy living creature. Children and adults will enjoy the sights,
sounds, and smells, and you'll never again take a bite of bread
for granted.

The mill is open Saturdays from 1:00 to 4:00 P.M. and Sundays
from 2:00 to 4:00 P.M., or call Kent Anderson at (206) 263–2273
to arrange a tour. Admission is free, and you may even be able to
take home a small bag of fresh milled flour, but donations are
always appreciated. To reach the mill, take the Interstate 5 exit 21
at Woodland just north of the Freeway, turn right at the first
stoplight, across the Lewis River toward Amboy. Bear left onto
Northeast Hayes Road, which becomes Cedar Creek Road. Turn
left in 9 miles onto Grist Mill Road; in 1 mile you will cross Cedar
Creek and see the mill on the bank. Be sure to thank the volunteers for their efforts before you leave.

Continue on to Amboy, then turn south on Highway 503
through picturesque lowlands of green fields and forests. In 7
miles turn left (east) on Northeast Lucia Falls Road and go 4½
miles to visit the **Pomeroy Living History Farm,** at 20902
Northeast Lucia Falls Road (206–686–3537). You can browse in
the British specialty shop, enjoy a spot of tea and English biscuits,
and on the first full weekend of each month from June through
October see the activities of a typical pre-electrical era Pacific
Northwest homestead farm. Costumed interpreters show visitors
how to grind corn and coffee, use a scrub board, feed and pet animals, use a crosscut logging saw, and conduct other daily tasks
from long ago. There is a beautiful herb garden next to the
kitchen and an operating blacksmith shop in the yard. The
Pomeroy Farm, now listed in the National Register of Historic
Places, was established in 1910 and preserved in the Pomeroy
family for generations, until it was opened to the public as a Living History Farm. There is a small fee for visiting the farm.

Continue south on Highway 503 to reach the town of Battle
Ground. Follow Main Street east through downtown to the

Lewis and Clark Railway Company, which offers excursion trains along the rushing Lewis River, past waterfalls, over a wooden trestle, and through a 340-foot tunnel, with a stop at Moulton Falls Park. Trains leave at 10:00 A.M. and 1:30 P.M. on Tuesdays and weekends during spring and October, and Monday through Saturday in the summer, with special holiday rides throughout the year. Dining service is offered Saturday evenings and Sunday mornings during the summer. Reservations are recommended. Call (206) 687–2626 or (503) 227–2626 for more information.

Heading east from Vancouver, Washington, you'll pass the towns of Camas and Washougal. These are mill towns that have recently become bedroom communities to the Portland area. Take the highway's business loop to explore the Camas downtown. Fourth Avenue is a pleasant walking street through the main commercial district. East of these communities the Columbia River Gorge becomes a National Scenic Area and the highway climbs 1,000 feet up the Columbia plateau at Cape Horn. From the top you'll enjoy an expansive view of the Gorge. On clear days this exhilarating vista stretches 30 or 40 miles. After descending back to river level, you may want to stop at the **Skamania General Store,** an old-style rural grocery, for a picnic lunch to enjoy at ⊃**Beacon Rock State Park** (509–427–8265). Beacon Rock is an 850-foot basalt tower, the remains of a volcano core, that served as a much welcomed sign to early river travelers that they had passed the difficult Cascade Rapids and faced no further obstructions to the Pacific Ocean 150 miles west. You can hike 1.2 miles through the forest to Hardy or Rodney falls, or for a breathtaking challenge climb the steep and narrow trail to the top of Beacon Rock itself. The park includes a beach from which you can view Pierce Island, an important wildlife preserve owned by the Nature Conservancy.

Just past Beacon Rock is the town of **North Bonneville,** where many of the Bonneville Dam employees live. This town was moved in 1976 when an expansion of the dam flooded its original location. The new town includes parks and 7 miles of bike paths. Until the river was dammed in the 1930s there were three rapids along this stretch of river, called the Upper, Middle, and Lower Cascades. These rapids made this an excellent salmon fishing ground, attracting natives from the coast to live for part of each year in villages and camps along the riverbank. During the ninteenth century, Fort Cascades was established just west of the rapids. You can visit the **Fort Cascades Historic Site,** which includes a 1.5-mile self-guided tour. Along the way you'll see prehistoric Indian petroglyphs, the original site of Fort Cascades (which burned during an attack in 1856), and artifacts from the colonial period when wagons and railroads were needed to portage around the rough water.

Water travel is easier now, even for huge barges that ply the Columbia, due to the network of dams and locks that begin with the ↄ**Bonneville Dam.** Visitors can tour the dam to see the huge electrical generators and the fish-ladder system that allows salmon and steelhead to migrate over the dam and continue up the river to spawn. The migration seasons of various species last almost continuously from mid-April through October. Visitors can view fish through huge underwater windows as they leap and swim dramatically upriver. On the Oregon side of the dam you can also see the locks in action, raising and lowering ships and barges.

Pampering and Outdoor Pleasure

The town of **Stevenson** is a bustling county seat, with many buildings dating back to the beginning of this century. Be sure to visit the ↄ**Columbia Gorge Interpretive Center** (turn left on Columbia, right on Vancouver Avenue), which includes artifacts, photographs, and memorabilia describing the region's history, all beautifully displayed. Call (509) 427–5141, extension 235, for information about the current center and the exciting new facility being developed right on the Columbia River's bank. Just east of Stevenson, the **Snug Harbor Lodge** (P.O. Box 882, Stevenson 98648) offers secluded riverfront hospitality in a home lovingly built by retired marine engineer Ross Humphreys. The lodge incorporates stone walls, mahogany trim, and ship hardware, including portholes. Guests can choose between the Admiral's Quarters and the Captain's Quarters, both of which offer great views. Breakfast and social activities are offered in the Officers' Mess. Snug Harbor's property includes private beaches and a boat dock. Call (509) 427–4287 for reservations.

Farther east from Stevenson, ↄ**Carson Hot Mineral Springs Resort** offers a healthful and charming opportunity to relax and be pampered. This is a classic mineral water spa that has changed little over the past century. For a moderate fee you can soak in huge claw-foot tubs, taking optional sips of the strong-tasting mineral water, then relax on a cot swaddled in sheets until all tensions have disappeared. Many visitors also enjoy a professional therapeutic massage. The historic hotel adjacent to the baths offers good food and inexpensive rooms, making a trip to Carson an ideal overnight holiday for Washington and Oregon residents. The hotel lobby is a meeting place where visitors can share a game of checkers and trade ideas on health and happiness. For questions or reservations write to Carson Hot Mineral Springs Resort at P.O. Box 370, Carson 98610, or call (509) 427–8292.

For more adventurous pleasure seekers there are public open-air hot spring pools on Forest Service property along the banks of the Wind River, accessible by a rough half-mile trail. To reach them, follow Highway 14 east, turn left on Berge Road, and continue onto Indian Cabin Road. Park at the end of the road. The parking area is privately owned so be prepared to pay a small parking fee. The Forest Service warns, "Do not be surprised if you find bathers taking advantage of the springs' privacy by indulging in nude bathing."

There are hundreds of miles of roads and trails in the Gifford Pinchot National Forest that covers the hills above the river. A good place to begin exploring this evergreen wonderland and learn more about the region's forests is the ⊃**Wind River Nursery and Arboretum,** one of the largest evergreen tree nurseries in the Northwest. To get there continue north on Wind River Road (Carson's main street) and follow direction signs. The short arboretum trail leads visitors past more than 200 species of trees from the world's temperate zones planted since 1912 to test their growing abilities in the Pacific Northwest. Many of the trees, which thrived at first, have long since died or remained stunted. Few have done as well as native trees or the towering redwoods introduced from California. It's an interesting introduction to forest ecology, the study of how trees adapt to a specific environment. Call the arboretum's visitors center at (509) 427–5645 for more information.

Farther east along the Columbia is the town of **Bingen,** and just up the hill is **White Salmon.** Until recently these were quiet riverside communities of hard-working old-timers, but they have become recreation meccas, especially for wind surfers. On summer weekends the beaches along this stretch of the Columbia are crowded board-to-board with enthusiasts, and the water is alive with colorful sails. **The Inn of the White Salmon** (172 West Jewett) is a charming spot for an overnight stay. Built in 1937 at the edge of this quaint hillside town overlooking the gorge, the hotel is now operated as a bed and breakfast with cozy, antique-decorated rooms and delicious breakfasts featuring European-style pastries, breads, and egg dishes. For reservations write to P.O. Box 1549, White Salmon 98672, or call (509) 493–2335.

Down the street, **Klickitat Pottery Shop** (264 Jewett Boulevard) is a fun place to browse and observe an ancient craft in action. Potter Edward Swick works in a wide-windowed studio on one side of the shop, churning out high-quality earthenware pieces for sale in the shop or on custom order. The graceful movements the potter uses to mold the clay is an enchanting dance, and the finished products are lovely to see and feel. For information, or to order a custom dinner set, write to P.O. Box 848, White Salmon 98672, or call (509) 493–4456.

Mount Adams Country

There is lots to see and do along the beautiful and relatively undiscovered White Salmon River Valley, which stretches from the Columbia River to Mount Adams. **Phil Zoller's Guide Service,** just north of mile marker 12, will raft you down the White Salmon or Klickitat rivers. It's an exhilarating experience. These are relatively easy rivers (Classes II to IV) suitable for families and beginners. The standard trip lasts three-and-one-half hours including the return by road to your starting point. Launchings are at 10:00 A.M. and 2:00 P.M. daily from March through October. Reservations are recommended, especially on summer weekends. Zoller offers other adventure options: moonlight cookout and float trips, fishing and scenic boat trips on the Columbia River, and winter Sno-Cat and snowmobile trips through the Mount Adams and Mount Simcoe backcountry. For information write to Zoller at Route 1, Box 522, White Salmon 98672, or call (509) 493–2641.

Our three-year-old son gave four stars to the ⊃**Peaceful Pastures Llama Ranch Bed and Breakfast** (1980 Highway 141, White Salmon 98672; 509–395–2786), 16 miles north of White

Salmon. There you'll find a herd of over 50 llama, wandering peacocks, rabbits, and the gracious hospitality of owners Jerry and Rebeka Stone. Their homestyle rooms offer stunning views of Mount Adams towering over green pastures and forests. After a satisfying breakfast, you can enjoy a pleasant stroll through pine forests and past bubbling creeks and serene ponds in the company of the Stones' gentle llama. Jerry and Rebeka's years of teaching experience make them excellent guides and hosts for visitors all ages.

Farther up Highway 141 at the base of Mount Adams you can enjoy mountain-view dining at **Serenity's Restaurant,** 1 mile south of Trout Lake. Everything about Serenity's is delightful, from the menu (a chatty newspaper called the *Territorial Times* that includes local history and suggestions for tourist activities) to daily specials and spectacular desserts. Specialties include fish such as fresh Rocky Mountain trout or baked Icelandic fillet and steaks. Adventurous diners can order a dinner for two with a "surprise entrée." There is a children's menu. Chef Earl Nordwall seldom misses the mark. Call (509) 395–2500 for reservations.

Trout Lake is a charming little community. The historic ↻**Trout Lake Country Inn** (15 Guler Road, Trout Lake, 98650), on the river one block off the main road, offers an old-fashioned soda fountain, bed and breakfast accommodations, and a family restaurant that sometimes features vaudeville and contemporary dinner theater. The classic Western false-front building has changed little since it was built in 1904. It served as the local store, post office, bathhouse, tavern, and gathering place for most of a century. The restaurant is open for lunch and dinner, with entertainment offered whenever inn owners Gil and Milly Martin can organize a show. These are community affairs, with over a dozen local residents performing, and everybody has a good time. Guest rooms are filled with charming antiques and offer beautiful mountain and river views. From the inn you can enjoy a pleasant stroll through town and forest, and in the evening you can curl up with a book in front of a blazing fire. Call (509) 395–2894 for reservations and theater schedules.

For more luxurious accommodations and excellent Northern Italian-style dinners, choose **Mio Amore Pensione** (P.O. Box 208, Trout Lake 98650; 509–395–2264), a European-style bed and breakfast inn and restaurant on six acres at the base of Mount Adams. Hosts Tom and Jill Westbrook offer the best of everything with generous style. Each guest room is different, designed on the theme of a Roman god or goddess: Vesta, goddess of the home; Bacchus, god of wine; Ceres, goddess of agriculture; and Venus, goddess of love and beauty. Tom is a skilled chef, specializing in the cuisine of Northern Italy, where he lived for several years. Reservations are required for dinner.

The Mount Adams area has an active volcanic history which has produced beautiful lava flows, caves, lava tubes, and other natural structures. Many caves in the area were once used by farmers in the days before refrigeration to store butter and cheese until they could get to market. These caves make the region popular with serious spelunkers (cave explorers), who approach the caverns with the same sense of challenge and caution that mountain climbers have for major peaks.

The **Ice Caves,** a series of lava tubes, are the easiest of the public caves to explore. Their name refers to columns (stalagmites) of ice that develop naturally in the lowest chamber during the winter. A century ago the giant icicles were harvested and sold in the Oregon towns of The Dalles and Hood River. The Forest Service has constructed a ladder leading down from the main entrance. A 120-foot tube that slopes southeastward is the most accessible part of the cave. Brave souls can explore four sinuous passages to the west, including a 200-foot tube that leads to a collapsed sink (a lower-level chamber). Near the base of the ladder, at the east end of the main section, a small opening leads to the low-arched Crack Room, named for small fissures that developed in the chamber floor. Farther up this passage is a natural bridge. In all there are about 650 feet of passages to explore. To reach the Ice Caves, follow Highway 141 5 miles west of Trout Lake and turn left at the sign. Be sure to bring warm clothes, boots, head protection, and dependable lights. Stop at the Mount Adams Ranger Station (509–395–2501), just north of Trout Lake, for more information and for directions to the Ice Caves, Big Lava Beds, Natural Bridges, huckleberry fields, and other local attractions.

The road east to Glenwood (turn right just after you cross the bridge north of Trout Lake) offers magnificent views of Mount Adams (called Pahto by native people) as you pass through the rich farmlands and climb hills above the White Salmon River Valley. Watch for the turnoff on your right to ⊃**Conboy Lake National Wildlife Refuge.** A 1-mile road takes you to the entrance, where you'll find brochures describing this wetland habitat. The Willard Springs Foot Trail, a 2½-mile loop with interpretive signs, is a pleasant way to learn more about the refuge's wildlife, including porcupines and wood ducks. The area was known as Tahk (Camas) Prairie to local tribes who relied on the abundant camas plants and waterfowl that thrived in this valley. Originally the valley was a wetland for much of the year, but over the past century farmers drained the lake, which decimated the wild camas beds and reduced the waterfowl populations. With half the area now a refuge and cooperative management by area farmers, wild camas plants are again common and bird populations have increased, especially those like Canada geese that enjoy fresh marshgrass shoots encouraged by continued haying.

Lands of Great Wonders

Some of the Columbia River Gorge's greatest wonders are now, tragically, flooded under the huge reservoirs behind Bonneville and The Dalles dams. Until 1957 the entire Columbia River cascaded over beautiful Celilo Falls. Native people had camped on this stretch of river for millennia, enjoying the area's abundant resources. Indians from throughout the region practiced traditional dip-net fishing from delicate pole platforms jutting bravely close to the swirling torrents. Tribal member George Silver Star described the scene: "The salmon struggle, almost swimming in the air, shaking off scales and river water." The area was also an important gathering place where tribes met to trade goods, enjoy festivities, and conduct peace councils. In 1805, explorer Meriwether Lewis described the Celilo Falls area as a "great emporium where all the neighboring nations assembled." Hundreds of the ancient pictographs (rock paintings) and petroglyphs (rock carvings) that once commemorated this life are now lost beneath the waters of the Columbia.

⊃**She-Who-Watches** (Tsagaglalal) is one of the most beautiful petroglyphs still visible, and an image that is often used on local tourism publicity. The original is located amid several petroglyphs at **Horsethief Lake State Park,** on the Columbia River opposite The Dalles. To find them, walk west from Horsethief Lake's south parking lot and look at the rocks above to your right. Note the different shapes; some are round like She-Who-

Watches while others are more angular, stick figures. This is believed to show the meeting of different tribes, each with their own artistic styles, at the important fishing grounds nearby. The park includes a sheltered bay with beaches that are great for swimming and fishing.

You'll find the darndest things along the Columbia River. Fifteen miles east of Horsethief Lake near the junction with Highway 97 is the Ɔ**Maryhill Museum** and a reproduction of England's **Stonehenge** monument, two legacies of eccentric millionaire Sam Hill. Maryhill (open daily from 9:00 A.M. to 5:00 P.M. from mid-March through mid-November) is a fine art museum filled with an eclectic collection that includes Rodin sculptures and watercolors, ninteenth-century French artwork, Russian icons, regional Indian art, the Queen of Romania's royal memorabilia, and a collection of chess sets. Cafe Maryhill, in the museum, serves deli-style lunches and snacks, with outdoor seating available overlooking the Columbia. The cement Stonehenge was created by Hill as a monument to soldiers killed during World War I, to remind us that "humanity is still being sacrificed to the god of war." (He believed that human sacrifices took place at the original Stonehenge in England.) Write to Maryhill Museum of Art, 35 Maryhill Museum Drive, Goldendale 98620, or call (509) 773–3733, for more information, including a calendar of upcoming shows and events.

The town of Goldendale, north of the Columbia on Highway 97, has been a prosperous commercial center for farmers since its inception. The town's well-kept homes and active downtown continue to emanate a friendly, self-sufficient atmosphere. For a historical perspective on the town, visit the **Klickitat County Historical Museum,** housed in the stately Presby Mansion on Broadway Street (Highway 142) and Grant Avenue. Touring this stylish house you'll feel as if you've stepped back in time a hundred years. Turn-of-the-century dolls left on the antique furniture give the impression that a child has just finished playing in the parlor, the kitchen looks as if someone is cooking dinner, the dining room table is set, period clothing is laid out in the bedrooms, and the mess in the kids' rooms suggests that some things never change. The museum is open from 9:00 A.M. to 5:00 P.M. daily, May to October, or by appointment during the off-season. There is a small admission fee. For more information call (509) 773–4303.

For an exhilarating look skyward, continue down Broadway Street and turn north on Columbus, past some of Goldendale's fine old homes. Follow signs uphill to ↺**Goldendale Observatory State Park,** where guides share their enthusiasm for the stars. Created and run by amateur astronomers, the observatory is unique for its accessibility to the public. During the day, you can view the sun using a special telescope, perhaps catching sight of a solar prominence—arcs of light and energy thousands of miles high. At night, the main 26-inch telescope brings galaxies and nebulae into view. The hilltop site itself provides great views of surrounding farmlands. The observatory is open from 1:00 to 5:00 P.M. and 7:00 to 11:00 P.M., Wednesday through Sunday, from April 1 through September 30. From October 1 through March 31, observatory hours are Friday, 7:00 to 9:00 P.M., Saturday, 1:00 to 5:00 P.M. and 7:00 to 9:00 P.M., and Sunday 1:00 to 5:00 P.M. Call (509) 773-3141 for more information.

The Lower Yakima Valley

Prosser has more to offer than you might expect for a quiet farm town. **Hinzerling Vineyard** (1520 Sheridan, Prosser 99350; 509–786–2163) is located in town at the corner of Wine Country Road and Sheridan. Founded in 1976 by the Wallace family, this is the oldest family-owned and operated winery in the Yakima Valley. Family members share their knowledge of wine production and samples of wines, including sweet dessert wines and dry Gewürztraminer. Down the road **Chinook Wines** (P.O. Box 387, Prosser 99350; 509–786–2725) has a friendly little tasting room in a small house just outside of town on Wine Country Road, a half mile east of exit 82 off Interstate 82. Owners Kay Simon and Clay Mackey gained extensive experience before embarking on the high art of fine wine production. Their wines are intended to complement Northwest cuisine. The Chinook sauvignon blanc is a perfect match for the native oysters and pink scallops of Puget Sound, their flavorful chardonnay will heighten the richness of Pacific salmon, and the merlot is ideal with eastern Washington spring lamb.

Hogue Cellars (P.O. Box 31, Prosser 99350; 509–786–4557), across Wine Country Road from Chinook Wines, offers gourmet pickled vegetables in addition to a wide selection of award-winning wines, including dry, sweet, and sparkling varieties. **Pontin Del Roza** (Route 4, Box 4735, Prosser 99350; 509–786–4449) is located at the corner of Hinzerling and McCreadie roads in the lovely hill district north of town. You can taste the Pontin family's special Roza sunset blush and Pinot gris. The **Yakima River Winery** (Route 1, Box 1657, Prosser 99350; 509–786–2805) is another small operation with a beautiful location, 2 miles out of town near the riverbank. The winery is especially proud of its barrel-aged red wines, including a cabernet sauvignon, merlot, Pinot noir, and Rendezvous. The winery also produces white and dessert wines. Each year the Yakima Winery sponsors educational events, allowing connoisseurs to taste a five-year "vertical" selection of vintages. To get there take Wine Country Road northwest from Prosser; just after you cross the Yakima River, turn left on North River Road, and watch for the winery on your right in about 2 miles.

Gourmet candies are another specialty you'll find near Prosser. The ↄ**Chukar Cherry Company** produces the fantastic Chocolate Chukars, a pitted, ripe, partly dried cherry (called a cherry raisin) dipped in chocolate to produce a royal taste treat. The Chukar Cherry Company gift shop, just west of town at 306 Wine Country Road, offers the best of the Yakima area's specialty foods, including dried cherries and berries, cherry preserves, and cherry sauces. For information call (509) 786–2055.

The **Benton County Historical Museum** (509–786–3842), at the Prosser City Park, is open Tuesday through Saturday from 10:00 A.M. to 4:00 P.M. and Sundays from 1:00 to 5:00 P.M. There's a little of everything, including natural history displays, an old-time general store counter, and "40 feet of gowns, 1843–1920," a selection of women's clothing styles of yesteryear. The real fun of this museum is to get the volunteers to share their stories of life in the valley years ago. You may hear memories of childhoods spent on farms, stories of small-town life, and the exploits of local celebrities.

A wonderful place to browse, eat, and spend the night in Prosser is the **Wine Country Inn** (104 Sixth Street, Prosser 99350), a beautifully restored and maintained historic house on the bank of the Yakima River. The gift shop features antiques, fine arts, and handcrafted gifts produced locally. The restaurant offers breakfast, afternoon tea, and gourmet dinners. Overnight guests have their choice of four rooms, including Riverside

Romance, from which you can enjoy a view of the river, and Aunt Nellie's, named after an early resident who would surely appreciate the antique furnishings and dainty floral motif. After a hard day of sightseeing, you can relax on the inn's cool deck, which juts over the river, and watch the sun set over the distant hills across the valley. The food is excellent, the service is friendly, and the wine is local. Life is good at the Wine Country Inn. Call (509) 786–2855 for reservations or more information.

Hangups, at 1130 Meade Avenue in downtown Prosser, is a delightful fine arts gallery owned and managed by the artists whose work is displayed. You'll find Frances Hawn's handwoven shawls, jackets, and scarves; insect-inspired enamel jewelry by Ed Klostermeyer (an entomology professor); fine woodwork by Elwin Riley; and abstract paper artworks by Patricia Proebsting. For more information about the artists and their gallery, call (509) 786–1149.

You can reach the town of Grandview by heading northwest from Prosser on Wine Country Road. The ⊃**Dykstra House Restaurant** (114 Birch Avenue, Grandview 98930), a National Historic Site built in the 1920s, offers delicious meals. The house, beautifully restored by owner Linda Williams, displays many fine antiques. Italian food is highlighted on Friday evenings, and Northwest cuisine is the specialty on Saturdays. The desserts are delicious, the produce is fresh, and the drinks (wine, beer, and fruit juice) include something special for every palate. If the weather is mild, you can savor your meal on the front porch. The restaurant is open Monday through Thursday from 9:30 A.M. to 4:30 P.M.; on Fridays from 9:30 A.M. to 4:30 P.M. and from 6:00 to 9:00 P.M.; and on Saturdays from 11:00 A.M. to 2:00 P.M. and from 6:00 to 9:00 P.M. Call (509) 882–2082 for reservations, which are recommended for Friday dinner and required on Saturday evenings.

Wine Country Road becomes Yakima Valley Highway northwest of Grandview because Sunnyside, a German Baptist colony at the turn of the century and nicknamed "Holy City," still has many residents who disapprove of alcoholic beverages. This did not discourage James and Geri Graves who, having traveled around the world and reached culinary peaks, chose Sunnyside as their retirement home, much to the town's benefit. A Cordon Bleu chef who served as assistant chef at New York's Waldorf-Astoria Hotel and as head chef at the Plaza, James Graves now maintains his own cooking school. With Geri's help he prepares reasonably priced seven course gourmet dinners on Friday and Saturday nights at ⊃**Le Ma Cuisine,** their little restaurant at the **Sunnyside Inn Bed and Breakfast.** The food is exquisite, the service is excellent, and the prices, though not cheap, are reasonable. The inn and restaurant are located at 800 East Edison in downtown Sunnyside 98944. Call (800) 221–4195 or (509) 839–5557 for reservations for this delightful dining experience.

South of Sunnyside, at the corner of Midvale and Emerald roads, you'll find the ⊃**Yakima Valley Cheese Company.** Visitors are welcome, Monday through Saturday from 9:30 A.M. to 5:00 P.M., to watch the process used to make award-winning European-style Gouda and Edam cheese. You can sample the company's specialty cheeses, such as hickory smoked, pompadour wheels (Gouda seasoned with herbs), black pepper Gouda, and Havarti. Most flavors are sold in eight- to ten-pound wheels, but small samples are also available. The gift shop also sells gourmet foods from the Yakima Valley. For information call (509) 837–6005.

For more off-the-beaten-path adventures, continue west on Emerald-Granger Road, a beautiful road that circles south of Snipes Mountain. When the road ends just outside of Granger, turn right onto Highway 223. From Granger, take Van Belle Road east for half a mile, then turn left on Beam Road and continue north 1½ miles to reach the ⊃**Granger Berry Patch Farm,** at 1731 Beam Road (800–346–1417 or 509–854–1413). The farm offers over twenty varieties of U-pick berries, a petting zoo, pumpkins, and Christmas trees in season. Berries are ripe from June through September, pumpkins are available during October, and berry jams are available year-round. The farm sponsors a berry festival the second and third weekends of July, a pumpkin festival each weekend in October, and a Christmas tree festival in December. Visitors are welcome to picnic on the grounds; be sure to bring bread or crackers on which to spread Granger Berry Patch Jam.

Native Lands and Stories

The Yakima Confederated Tribes and Bands is one of the largest self-governing Native American Nations. The Yakima Indian Reservation includes a portion of the lower Yakima Valley and

119

much of the scrub-steppe and pine-forest covered hills farther south. The town of **Toppenish** is located on the reservation in a wide, fertile part of the Valley. The town's name, which means "sloping and spreading land" in the Yakima language, aptly describes the ancient lake bed that forms the broad plain on which it sits. In recent years Toppenish's downtown has been renovated to emphasize Western-style false-front stores and classic turn-of-the-century brick buildings. A walking tour of downtown reveals galleries, antique shops, tourist cafes, and a colorful array of large outdoor murals depicting the area's history, including "When Hops Were Picked by Hand"; "The Rhythms of Celilo," a view of Indians fishing at Celilo Falls on the Columbia River; and "Hot and Dusty Work," a cattle-branding scene.

These murals have been created with the help of the Toppenish Mural Society, which reviews artists' proposals to ensure that subjects are historically accurate and consistent with the town's standards. The society sponsors Mural-in-a-Day events, organizing teams of artists who work together to execute a new masterpiece within the one-day time limit. The society maintains an inventory of suitable walls around town and makes arrangements between artists and building owners. During the mural season, from April through October, visitors to Toppenish have a good chance of seeing a mural being created.

Residents of the area cooperate and compete at the **Toppenish Pow-Wow and Rodeo,** held the first weekend in July. This is not the only professional rodeo in Washington, nor is it the only powwow, but this is the only joint powwow and rodeo and an excellent chance to absorb a balance of western American culture. For more information about this and other interesting local events, write to the Toppenish Chamber of Commerce at P.O. Box 28, Toppenish 98948, or call (509) 865–3262.

To learn more about Native American culture, visit the ⊃**Yakima Nation Cultural Heritage Center,** on Highway 97 (P.O. Box 151, Toppenish 98948; 509–865–2800). From a distance you'll spot the colorful peaked roof of the center's Winter Lodge, modeled after the ancestral A-shaped homes of the Yakima tribes. The impressive Yakima Nation Museum is the highlight of the center. Beautiful museum exhibits describe the history and traditions of the Yakima tribes. A large, angular tule (reed) lodge at the center of the museum shows how extended families lived during the winter. Sweat lodges made from earth, branches, and

Yakima Nation Cultural Heritage Center Campground

animal skins tell of physical and spiritual purification. Dioramas depict daily Indian life of centuries ago. You can see a woman's "time ball," with which she recorded meaningful events in her life using knots, beads, and string. You can also learn the story of Spilyay, the trickster often seen in the guise of coyote, who taught humanity how to live in harmony with the natural world. Other exhibits describe how the Yakima were conquered and give personal accounts by tribal members who were removed from their families as children and forced to attend military-style boarding schools where they were forbidden to speak their native language or learn traditional skills. The museum is open daily from 10:00 A.M. to 5:00 P.M. and there is a small admission charge.

At the center's gift shop adjacent to the museum, you can purchase beautiful local beadwork and other Native American art and cultural items. The **Heritage Inn Restaurant,** also part of the tribal center, offers delicious meals, including Yakima tribal favorites such as barbecued salmon, buffalo stew, Indian fry bread, and huckleberry desserts. The restaurant is open Monday to Wednesday and for Sunday brunch from 8:00 A.M. to 2:00 P.M., and Thursday to Saturday from 8:00 A.M. to 8:00 P.M. Call (509) 865–2551 for reservations. The center maintains an extensive library on Native American history and culture. There is also a luxury campground with recreation center and swimming pool where, in addition to more conventional camping facilities, you can rent a tepee with room for a whole family. The tepees are constructed in the traditional manner used for generations by the Yakima people, but as a concession to modern comfort and convenience they are set on a cement floor and have cots for sleeping.

Twenty-five miles west of the Yakima Indian Tribal Center in the heart of the reservation is ⊃**Fort Simcoe State Park Heritage Site.** It's a lovely park with ancient oak shade trees, a lush green lawn, and a dozen restored buildings filled with period furnishings. The fort is located on a traditional native village site where the ancient Mool Mool bubbling springs have created a beautiful oasis of reed-filled wetlands surrounded by woods. In summer, you may catch sight of green and pink Lewis's Woodpeckers, which breed in abundance in the ample Garry oak stands. The park, a popular picnic spot for local residents, features plenty of shade trees, running water, and an adventure playground.

Considering that this state park is located within the reservation, the interpretive center gives a surprisingly one-sided portrait of Fort Simcoe's history. Displays euphemistically state that the fort was established to "protect" reservation residents, and later, as a boarding school run by Methodist missionaries, provided "services" to reservation Indians. There is no mention of abuses the Yakima people endured at the hands of colonists, treaty promises broken by Governor Stevens, injustices committed against peaceful Indians during the "Indian Wars," or the systematic destruction of tribal culture by missionaries, who forbade young children to learn traditional skills or even speak their native language. We recommend that visitors to this interpretive center also tour the Yakima Tribal Museum described earlier for balance.

Park grounds are open daily from April 1 through September 30 and on weekends and holidays from October 1 through March 31. From October to March, the historical buildings and interpretive center are open only by appointment. For more information write to Fort Simcoe State Park, 5150 Fort Simcoe Road, White Swan 98952, or call (509) 874–2372 .

The **Toppenish National Wildlife Refuge** is located off Highway 97 south of Toppenish. The refuge's marshlands and thick riverside forests are excellent places to view the fall and spring migrations of Canada geese and ducks such as grebes, teals, scaups, and pintails. There are bald eagles, prairie falcons, and other wildlife that once populated the entire Yakima Valley area.

Land of Abundance

A 10-mile signed "Fruit Loop" route that circles the orchard-covered hills above the town of ⊃Zillah is an ideal way to discover the valley's agricultural opulence. To visit Zillah take Interstate 82, exit 52 or 54, or follow the Yakima Valley Highway from Sunnyside through Granger and turn left onto Zillah's First Avenue. The loop starts from the downtown tourist information office at the corner of First Avenue and Fifth Street, where you can pick up a route map during office hours, or just follow the colorful signs from downtown north on Roza Drive and left onto the Yakima Valley Highway. Along the way you'll enjoy beautiful views of the lower valley's patchwork quilt of farms, and will pass by Zillah Oaks, Bonair, Hyatt Vineyards, Covey Run, Portteus, Horizon's Edge, and Eaton Hill wineries.

123

Of course, every winery claims to offer the best product, so it's up to you to determine your favorites. Each has a tasting room where visitors are offered a small sample of the many vintages available. Don't feel shy if you're not a connoisseur; winery staff will share their knowledge and offer suggestions for the best wine for various occasions. If you enjoy a particular vintage, you can purchase a few bottles to take home. Most tasting rooms also sell nonalcoholic drinks, snacks, and gifts. Many wineries welcome visitors to picnic on their grounds, so you may want to assemble a basket of snacks before embarking on your wine-sampling adventure.

If wine tasting has given you an appetite and you forgot the picnic basket, you'll want to eat at ꓛ**El Ranchito** (509–829–5880), the most authentic Mexican restaurant, bakery, and specialty store you are likely to find in Washington state, located at 1319 East First Avenue, the last stop on the Fruit Loop tour. It has an informal atmosphere where farm-worker families, local professionals, and tourists all enjoy fresh tamales, burritos, tostadas, and guava or mango fruit juice. In warm weather the shaded patio makes an especially pleasant place to eat. You can also buy Mexican art and household goods, including *boda y religiosos* (religious goods), *pan dulce* (sweet bakery goods), and *discos y cartuchos* (Spanish records and tapes).

For a nostalgic visit to an old-fashioned country store and orchard, stop by **Donald Fruit and Mercantile,** just east of Interstate 82 at exit 44 on Donald–Wapato Road. The building was constructed in 1911 and still has a wood floor and most of the original store fixtures. Out front you'll see a selection of fresh fruit and vegetables in season. Inside you'll find a little of everything, with emphasis on turn-of-the-century household items and toys, fruit juices, candy, and locally produced specialty foods. Adjacent to the store is an orchard of antique variety apple trees, which visitors are welcome to explore. In the autumn, when they are ripe, you can taste the unique flavors of these old-style fruit. Donald Fruit and Mercantile is open 9:00 A.M. to 6:00 P.M. daily from May through December. Call (509) 877–3115 for more information.

Near Wapato you'll find the beautiful **Staton Hills Winery,** where owner Peter Ansdell prides himself on using the most innovative techniques to grow premium grapes and produce excellent wines. Visitors can see up-to-date viticulture (grape

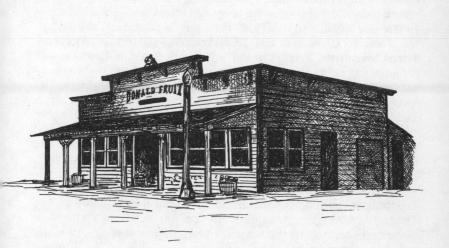

Donald Fruit and Mercantile

growing) using three types of advanced trellising: the Guyot, the gable trellis, and the Tatura trellis, all designed to help the new grape leaves get maximum sunlight. The beautiful French country-style winery built of local stone and cedar has a wine-tasting room, gift shop, and sophisticated wine processing facilities, which use oak barrels imported from France and Germany as well as modern stainless steel equipment. To reach the Staton Hills Winery, take Highway 12 east from Interstate 82 exit 40, follow the road as it curves left to become Thorp Road, then turn right onto Gangl Road. For information contact Staton Hills, 71 Gangl Road, Wapato 98951, or call (509) 877–2112.

Just south of Yakima is the town of Union Gap, the single gap in the line of hills that divides the upper and lower Yakima Valley. Next to the gap is the ↄ**Central Washington Agricultural Museum,** located in Fulbright Park. Visitors can examine an amazing collection of farm machinery and hear from volunteer curators about the lives and fortunes of valley farmers. The large equipment is arranged outdoors on spiral terraces in a surreal mechanical parade around a windmill tower situated higher on the hill. You'll see horse-drawn plows and mowers, huge old steam tractors, antique threshers, and hop harvesters. Inside the buildings are additional displays of farm equipment, hand tools, and household goods.

A portion of Fulbright Park is farmed using some of the old equipment, which is maintained in working condition by the Central Washington Antique Farm Equipment Club. Visitors are sometimes treated to the scene of working horse teams plowing museum fields or an old steam harvester in use. The Pioneer Power Show, held in mid-August, attracts farm equipment collectors from around the state to enjoy antique tractor pulls, grain milling, a starlight parade of old motorized equipment, and a chance to demonstrate the use of antique hand tools and household gadgets. To get to the museum from Union Gap, follow Main Street south 2 miles and across the Highway 97 overpass to the Fulbright Park turnoff. For information call (509) 457–8735 or (509) 248–0432.

If you follow Ahtanum Road 15 miles west from downtown Union Gap, past farms and small ranches, between sagebrush-covered hills into the narrow and fertile Ahtanum Valley, and past the little town of Ahtanum itself, you'll reach the historic ↄ**Ahtanum Mission.** It's a beautiful site: green lawns with picnic tables, a meandering creek in the shade of ancient oaks, and some of the state's oldest apple trees still grow in the quiet orchard. A log cabin church, built in 1867, sits quietly by the creek. The site has a dramatic and tragic history that contrasts with its current serenity. The original mission was established by French Oblate missionaries in 1847 as one of the first missions in the region. According to pioneer writer John Lynch, "Ahtanum was the cradle and the proving ground of irrigation in the State of Washington." But the missionaries succeeded too well in establishing trust and friendship with local tribes; in 1853, U.S. troops burned the mission because they suspected the fathers of supporting the Indians in conflicts with whites. The mission park is still owned by the Catholic Church, and services are held at the Old Saint Joseph Church during the summer. You can tour the tiny building when it is not in use. Visitors pay a small fee to picnic or camp at the site.

The Upper Yakima Valley

The city of Yakima offers delightful activities little-known to outsiders. Walking or bicycling along the 10-mile ⊃**Yakima Greenway** trail system is the perfect way to enjoy the Yakima River environment. The path stretches from the quiet town of Selah at the north, past several riverfront parks, to the 70-acre **Yakima Arboretum** at the south end (near the intersection of Interstate 82 and Nob Hill Boulevard). The arboretum includes hiking trails, a Japanese garden, picnic areas, fountains, and the new Jewett Interpretive Center.

The best way to explore downtown is on the free trolleys that ply Yakima's inner-city streets. The Red Line travels east-west on Yakima Avenue. The Green Line goes north-south along First Street. Watch for the old-style trolleys, complete with oak paneling, decorated glass windows, brass hardware, and a clanging bell. Railroad themes permeate Yakima. Along the old railroad line through downtown you'll find the renovated North Front Street district, with its interesting businesses and activities. Nothing will delight a beer connoisseur more than visiting **Grant's Brewery,** America's oldest brew pub, which occupies the historic Yakima Train Depot. Even if beer is not your drink, you can enjoy a light meal and either hard or soft cider. Grant's Brewery is open daily.

Wine aficionados will enjoy Front Street's **Thurston Wolfe Winery & Tasting Room,** offering a selection of premium table wines, champagnes, and dessert wines produced on the premises. If you're still hungry there is the **Greystone Restaurant,** featuring gourmet dinners and classic dining elegance. For more casual eating, **Deli de Pasta,** a small Italian restaurant in the old Longbranch Saloon, offers pasta products and sauces made from scratch in the kitchen. For health's sake, owner and chef Diane Traner uses only the finest ingredients, a minimum of salt, and no preservatives. There is a selection of both local and Italian wines.

Just south of the main railroad line is **Track 29,** a charming shopping center made up of 21 railroad cars parked on tracks as if about to carry visitors off to distant lands. Track 29 solves the problem that Yakima businessman and train lover John Edwards encountered when he purchased more rail cars than he knew what to do with. Although Edwards originally planned to house just his own fruit company, the project grew to include sixteen businesses. With the help of architect Ron Cameron, Track 29 developed around a Victorian village theme. You can buy jewelry in an old passenger car, have lunch in a caboose, or browse through a variety of specialty shops.

A trip on the ⊃**Yakima Interurban Trolley Line** is an ideal way for visitors to explore some of Yakima's less-traveled highlights. The trolley travels through downtown city streets, along the Yakima River, across the Naches River, and past Convicts' Cave, a hillside quarry where convicts once worked, on the way to the town of Selah. The system was owned by the Union Pacific Railroad as part of 43 miles of trolley and freight lines operated in the Yakima area during the first half of the century. The rail rights-of-way and trolley cars were donated by Union Pacific to the city in 1985. Now, more than 80 volunteers serve as drivers, conductors, and tour guides to keep the trolley system running. The four currently operating trolleys, built in the 1920s and '30s, are stored in the trolley barn at South Third Avenue and Pine Street. The barn includes a trolley and rail museum, with a belt-driven machine shop that is still used to maintain the trolleys. Public rides are offered Saturdays, Sundays, and holidays from May through mid-October, leaving Yakima at 10:00, 12:00, 2:00, and 4:00, and leaving Selah at 11:00, 1:00, 3:00, and 5:00. Evening rides are offered weekdays during July and August, leaving Yakima at 6:30 and 8:00 P.M. and departing from Selah at 7:15. For information call (509) 575–1700.

Two miles east of Yakima is ⊃**Birchfield Manor Restaurant and Bed and Breakfast,** which offers elegant meals and overnight accommodations in a beautiful 23-room Victorian-style mansion, complete with crystal chandeliers, a winding staircase, and flower garden. You'll find an abundance of comforts (hot tub, pool, private baths) and a choice of five charming, antique-filled guest rooms. Dinners, served Thursday through Saturday, are exceptional, prepared by chef and co-owner Wil Masset. If you are in doubt about the best wine to choose, ask for a tour of the manor's wine cellar, where Masset will offer recommendations from available vintages. Because of the restaurant's limited seating, reservations are required. The Birchfield is located at 2018 Birchfield Road, off Highway 24 in Yakima 98901. Call (509) 452–1960.

The ⊃**Desert Rose,** hosted by Pete and Grace Optekar, is a bed and breakfast guest house near the small community of Moxee in the wheat-growing hills above Yakima. This English country manor-style home has a graceful circular staircase and an abundance of hand-rubbed oak furniture. The rooms are beautiful and the food is sumptuous. From its hilltop location, visitors can see the tip of Mount Rainier and enjoy night views of Yakima's city lights. Three hundred annual days of clear skies and its rural location make the Desert Rose an ideal location for stargazing, and the Optekars share their eight-inch Celestron telescope with guests who wish to explore the universe. Guests can also enjoy hiking, bird-watching, hunting, and fishing, and the Optekars recommend that you bring your horse (there's plenty of room in the corrals) or a mountain bike to explore the many miles of trails. For information write the Desert Rose at 18190 Highway 24, Moxee 98936, or call (509) 452–2237.

Highway 12 west of Yakima passes through the orchard-filled Naches Valley. At the entrance to this valley you can visit the ancient ⊃**Indian Painted Rocks** petroglyphs. A short hike up the hillside trail takes you to sheer rock walls where images painted by the valley's original inhabitants are still visible. You'll also enjoy beautiful views of the two fertile valleys stretching below. To reach the site, take Highway 12 west toward White Pass. At the 199-mile post, turn left on Ackley Road, then take an immediate right and park on the shoulder of the road near the large historical marker sign.

Just past the Naches Valley, 2 miles west of the Highway 410 turnoff, is the **Oak Creek Wildlife Area,** a feeding station for elk, deer, and mountain goats in winter and a popular spot for hunting and bird-watching. Continuing west you'll ascend the Tieton River and climb through sagebrush-covered hills and the Gifford Pinchot National Forest up to White Pass. Along the way you'll pass numerous lakes, fishing resorts, and campgrounds. It's a spectacular route surrounded by dramatic geology and forest-covered mountains. White Pass has relatively light traffic and long stretches of undeveloped forest, making it a favorite route for bicyclists and a popular destination for outdoor recreation.

Off the Beaten Path in Northeast Washington

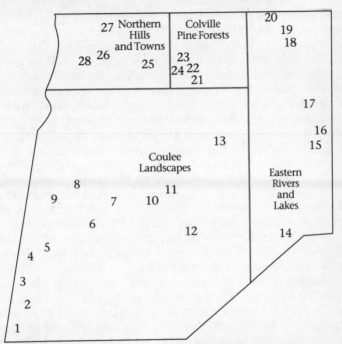

1. Pioneer Village
2. Soap Lake
3. Lake Lenore Caves
4. Dry Falls Interpretive Center
5. Coulee City
6. Bubba's Almira Steakhouse
7. Keller's Ferry
8. Colville Tribal Cultural Museum and Gift Shop
9. Steamboat Rock
10. Seven Bays
11. Fort Spokane
12. Lincoln County Historical Museum
13. Silver Beach Resort
14. Spokane River Centennial Trail
15. Pend Oreille County Historical Museum
16. Pioneer Park
17. Manresa Grotto
18. Sullivan Lake
19. Washington Hotel
20. Gardner Cave
21. Roadhouse Restaurant
22. My Parent's Estate Bed and Breakfast
23. Kettle Falls Historical Center
24. Twin Springs Farm
25. Sherman Pass Scenic Byway
26. Triangle J Ranch Hostel and Bed and Breakfast
27. Curlew
28. Stonerose Interpretive Center

Northeast Washington

Washington's northeast corner is a land of stark contrasts. In a few hours you can travel through steep basalt canyons thick with the spicy smell of sagebrush, over hills covered with wheat field and dotted with farms, and through thick pine forests. The region's geological history is dynamic and readily visible in the layer-cake walls of coulees, the steep canyons cut deep through solidified lava by ancient glaciers and rivers. You'll see the restless passage of time written in stone as you travel along the region's byways. Many of the roads themselves are ancient pathways traveled on for centuries by people and animals. You'll find several excellent interpretive centers to help you appreciate northeast Washington's exciting past as you revel in its present beauty.

Spend some time meeting small-town residents at a cafe lunch counter or tavern. The people of this region are close to the earth, daily aware of their relationship to the farms, forests, and rivers upon which so much of the local economy depends. They take pride in their Native American, farmer, rancher, and lumberman heritage, which is very much alive in the current culture. You'll find communities working to preserve historic tribal campsites, railway junctions, farms, gold mining, and logging towns in order to help remember their roots.

Northeast Washington is a favorite area for people who enjoy outdoor activities, including hiking, bicycling, fishing, hunting, and boating. There are hundreds of square miles of national forest crossed with countless dirt roads and trails. On the shores of many rivers and lakes, you will find secluded retreats and fishing resorts where local sportsmen and sportswomen rub shoulders with visitors from around the world.

Coulee Landscapes

A good place to start your tour is the town of Ephrata. From Interstate 90, take Highway 283 northeast from George or Highway 17 northwest from Moses Lake. You'll cross field upon circular field of corn, wheat, potatoes, and legumes kept green by massive central-pivot irrigation systems. This plain is so wide you can glimpse hills to the north but only a hint of a southern ridge. Like many northeast Washington towns, Ephrata preserves its past in a local historical museum. Grant County's ⊃**Pioneer Village,** located east of the highway at the far end of town, provides a three-dimensional view of pioneer life. Visitors walk through carefully re-created print, camera, and blacksmith shops, saloons, a one-room schoolhouse, and homesteads. Outside is a collection of the big farm machines that made Grant County a major agricultural producer. The museum is open from early May to mid-September, 10:00 A.M. to 5:00 P.M. Monday through Saturday, 1:00 to 4:00 P.M. on Sundays, and is closed on Wednesdays. For more information contact the Pioneer Village and Museum, Grant County Historical Society, 742 Basin Street North (P.O. Box 1141, Ephrata 98823; 509–754–3334). For another glimpse of local history you can see the **Grant County Courthouse,** west of the highway at the corner of First NW and C Streets, built in 1917 and heated geothermally from a nearby hot spring.

Follow Highway 28 north to ⊃**Soap Lake.** Cherished by local tribes and early settlers for its healing properties, Soap Lake continues to draw people seeking rejuvenation from its buoyant waters. Seventeen minerals, with sodium bicarbonate the most common, give the water its soapy texture, although the frothy piles of suds that once accumulated on the lakeshore have disappeared due to dilution from irrigation. The popularity of this resort town is nothing like its heyday at the turn of the century, but the crowds still come. You can experience the water's effects with daily soaks at one of the town's two beaches or in baths piped from deep in the lake to several of the town's motels. Soaking in the healthful mineral water in the privacy of your own room is a wonderful luxury. Both public beaches are crowded in summer when water temperatures can reach as high as 100 degrees Fahrenheit. West Beach, located near the highway and motels, is the most popular with tourists. East Beach, separated by a small, rocky peninsula, is preferred by local residents and has a diving float. It also has showers, helpful for removing the water's alkaline residue.

Notaras Lodge (P.O. Box 987, Soap Lake 98851; 509–246–0462), on Main Avenue one block south of the lake, is the most unusual of the Soap Lake resort motels. Each room is decorated according to local historical themes. One highlights the colorful personality of the town's first woman mayor, who served during the 1940s; another celebrates local families of Greek descent, including those of the owners. Considerable artistic creativity and craftsmanship goes into each room. The generous-size bathtubs include three spigots: hot, cold, and Soap Lake mineral water. Lodge owner Marina Romary also runs **Don's Restaurant** across the street (14 Canna Street; 509–246–1217), a local favorite for steak and seafood. Don's is open for lunch Monday through Friday, and dinner is served daily, with delicious Greek specialties featured on Mondays and Fridays.

Soap Lake is the southernmost of the Grand Coulee's chain of mineral-rich lakes. The Grand Coulee was formed by glacial action that cut through layers of thick volcanic basalt. Highway 17 from Soap Lake to Coulee City provides a breathtaking route through the lower end of the coulee. You'll follow secluded lake beds, cut deep into reddish brown cliffs, their shorelines often crusted white with minerals. Lake Lenore has excellent public access, with several spots to put in a boat or to stop and watch the varied waterfowl in grassy lakeside wetlands.

Off the highway opposite Lake Lenore is the turnoff to ⊃**Lake Lenore Caves.** A gravel road, open 10:00 A.M. to 6:00 P.M. daily, takes you to the trailhead for a short hike through wonderful-smelling sagebrush, up the cliffsides to the ancient caves. There, like generations of hunter-gatherers before, you can find shelter from the heat in these cool, rocky overhangs. Watch the graceful swooping of cliff swallows, listen to crickets, hear the dry scrub rustling in the breeze, and absorb the stark beauty of the coulee landscape framed before you by the cave's jagged stones. It's a good place to meditate on the powerful glacial meltwaters that created the coulees and to imagine the lives of ancient people who used these caves for protection from their harsh environment.

Between Alkali and Blue lakes you can catch sight of the **Caribou Cattle Trail.** A roadside sign marks the point where the trail crosses the road. Originally a native path, the 500-mile trail was used in the late nineteenth century as a supply route by miners and Blue Lake homesteaders. A few miles north, on Blue Lake, **Coulee Lodge Resort** (HCR 1, Box 156, Coulee City 99115–9608; 509–632–5565) offers lakeside cabins, campsites, swimming, sandy beaches, boat rentals, and a general store. Nearby, **Sun Lakes State Park** has lakeside camping with similar amenities, plus horseback riding, golf, and road access to the floor of Dry Falls.

The ⊃**Dry Falls Interpretive Center,** open 10:00 A.M. to 6:00 P.M. in summer and located just east of the highway, offers spectacular views of what was once a gigantic waterfall. Exhibits explain the dynamic forces that created this massive precipice and why it is now without water. You'll learn of the lush environment that covered this area 20 million years ago during the Miocene Epoch and how the largest basaltic lava flows on earth, up to a mile thick, eventually engulfed 200,000 square miles of the Pacific Northwest. Powerful forces buckled and warped the cooled lava plateau, followed by glaciation and massive flooding, creating the dramatic landscape before you.

Highway 2 crosses the Dry Falls Dam at the south end of Banks Lake. Turn right off Highway 2 at ⊃**Coulee City** to explore this windblown Western town, originally a watering hole along the Caribou Trail. Huge grain elevators now dominate downtown. For information on the town's history, pick up a walking-tour brochure at the friendly **Country Mall Store,** on Main Street next to four shady cottonwood trees. If you happen into town on a Tuesday, you can learn about art and local history from members of the **Highlighters Art Club,** who meet at their gallery on Main between Fifth and Sixth. This good-humored group, ranging from children to old-timers in their eighties, encourages local artists and collects their work. The gallery, in a building constructed in 1905, features the varied work of eight local artists and is open from 1:00 to 4:00 P.M. Wednesday to Saturday, May through September.

As you continue east, Highway 2 passes through a series of small farm towns at 10-mile intervals. If you hanker for a hearty meal, stop at ⊃**Bubba's Almira Steakhouse,** at 218 West Main in Almira, two blocks south of the highway. Here, Tom and Sue Biss cook up 22-ounce steaks two inches thick as well as sumptuous chicken, lamb, and lobster tail with wild rice pilaf and vegetable dishes, all made from scratch. They offer lighter fare, too, including crunchy sweet-pea salads, homemade New England-style chowder and numerous hamburger variations. You can indulge in Bubba's beloved mud pies smothered in hot fudge or the "best cheesecakes west of New York." Bubba's is open daily for dinner. Call (800) 400–0176 or (509) 639–0176 for reservations.

From Almira, continue east on Highway 2 across more wheat-covered expanses to the pleasant farm town of **Wilbur.** For a spectacular taste of Washington's varied topography, head north from Wilbur on Highway 21. You'll travel past trees and farms in distant clumps like islands in a sea of grain before the road winds abruptly down through layered coulee cliffs to the Columbia River. **Keller's Ferry Landing** resort (P.O. Box 5, Coulee Dam 98116; 800–648–LAKE from Washington and British Columbia, or 509–633-0201) has sandy beaches, boat rentals, launches, and campsites along the shore. There are also several boat-in campsites to the east.

⊃**Keller's Ferry** is a free ten-minute crossing with runs every fifteen minutes between 6:00 A.M. and 11:00 P.M. Unlike the ferries that ply the Northwest coast, this is no mighty ship. Yours may be the only car on the ferry's small deck. The river is often so placid you can see the dry sage-covered cliffs and hills reflected in the water for a doubly beautiful view. From the northern landing you can turn left on Swawilla Basin Road to the Grand Coulee Dam or continue north on scenic Highway 21 up the Sanpoil River to the old mining town of Republic (described later in the section on Northern Hills and Towns). The 24-mile road west toward Grand Coulee Dam is a hilly one, surrounded by ponderosa pine, wild roses, purple lupine, and woolly mullein, with occasional old barns and glacial erratics along the way. You may even spot a bear cub or mule deer exploring the dry roadside. The Grand Coulee Dam is 4 miles south of the junction with Highway 155.

In East Coulee Dam, turn left at Birch Street to visit the ⊃**Colville Tribal Cultural Museum and Gift Shop,** at 516 Birch Street (509–633–0751), open 10:00 A.M. to 6:00 P.M. daily during summer. The museum recounts the story of tribal life when the salmon swam free before the Columbia River was dammed. Exhibits feature ancient fishing scenes, tribal lodges, and tepees as well as cedar and beargrass basket displays. The gift shop highlights beadwork, paintings, prints, and ceramics by local native artists and tribespeople as well as Pendleton, Perce, and Navajo blankets. Staff members are on hand to answer questions and let you know about other Colville tribal enterprises. They can describe how to get to the grave site of the legendary Nez Perce leader Chief Joseph, buried in exile on a hillside northeast of Nespelem, 13 miles north on Highway 155.

In contrast to the "before" picture glimpsed at the museum, you can stop by the **Grand Coulee Dam Visitor Arrival Center** across the bridge to learn the story of the world's largest concrete structure, celebrated in Woody Guthrie's famous song

"Roll On Columbia" and the largest component of the Pacific Northwest's extensive hydroelectric system. Exhibits at the visitors center explain the dam's history and engineering. You can also tour the dam itself, walking through chambers above huge generators, each of which produces enough electricity for a good-size town. The center is open daily from 8:30 A.M. until after the evening laser light show from Memorial Day through September, and 9:00 A.M. until 5:00 P.M. October through May. The forty-minute light show of animated graphics projected on the dam's surface runs at 10:00 P.M. Memorial Day weekend through July, 9:30 P.M. in August, and 8:30 P.M. in September. For more information contact the Grand Coulee Project Office, Code 140, P.O. Box 620, Grand Coulee 99133; (509) 633–9503.

Visitors to the Grand Coulee area can enjoy the extensive **Community Trail** system that connects all four towns (West and East Coulee Dam, Grand Coulee, and Electric City), and offers exercise and spectacular views. The **Down River Trail,** a 6½-mile hiking, biking, wheelchair-accessible path, follows the Columbia River north from the dam. With gentle grades and landscaped rest stops, both trails offer relaxing strolls.

Within walking distance of the dam on a quiet residential hillside to the west is Coulee Dam's only bed and breakfast, **Four Winds Guest House** (301 Lincoln Street, Coulee Dam 99116; 800–786–3146). Built as a boardinghouse in the 1930s during the dam's construction period, the Four Winds building served many purposes until hosts Dick and Fe Taylor refurbished the house and grounds in 1986. The Guest House now offers ten large rooms decorated in 1930s style, each focused on an aspect of the area's people and history. Four Winds does not allow smoking, children under eight, or pets. For information on other places to stay, contact the Grand Coulee Dam Area Chamber of Commerce at (509) 633–3074.

Highway 155 follows the eastern shore of Banks Lake back to Coulee City. It is preferable to drive south on this road so you can easily pull over at viewpoints and appreciate the magnificence of the geology and wildlife. ⊃**Steamboat Rock,** a former island in an ancient river bed, rises like a solidified wave from the lake's north end. Picturesque **Northrup Canyon Trail** begins at the end of a half-mile road across the highway from the rest stop near Steamboat Rock's north end. This moderately difficult trail stretches from a sheltered canyon, through rare forests, and up a steep path to Northrup Lake atop the gorge. You'll see remnants of the area's first settlers along the way, including old homestead buildings and a stagecoach road on the canyon's south side, and perhaps view eagles soaring overhead.

Steamboat Rock State Park offers day-use facilities at the base of the mesa's south end for swimming and picnics. Reservations are recommended for summer stays since this is one of the state's more popular campsites. A hiking trail to the rock's 640-acre summit offers excellent views of the surrounding terrain. Be sure to bring water and wear good boots or walking shoes. Keep your distance from the edge of the cliff since basalt breaks easily, and though rattlesnakes in the area aren't considered particularly aggressive or lethal, a bite is still painful and dangerous. For more information on trails or campsites, contact Steamboat State Park, P.O. Box 370, Electric City 99123–0370, or call (509) 633–1304 during business hours, May 1 through Labor Day.

The town of **Creston,** east of Wilbur on Highway 2, begins and ends in wheat fields. The nearby crest of the Columbia Plateau, for which Creston is named, was known by local tribes as "The Place Where Deer Dry Their Antlers." It's still common to see mule deer loping through the fields. Take the left fork 2 miles east of Creston to reach Seven Bays and Fort Spokane. Bachelor Drive (Miles Creston Road) zigzags through a narrow, wooded valley back to rolling wheat fields before it descends into pine forests near Lake Roosevelt, the huge reservoir behind the Grand Coulee Dam.

⊃**Seven Bays** is a modern resort owned by the Colville Confederated Tribe along the largely undeveloped Lake Roosevelt shoreline. You'll find a hilltop campground as well as a marina, boat rental, ranger station, store, and restaurant open Sunday through Thursday from 9:00 A.M. to 7:00 P.M. and Friday and Saturday from 8:00 A.M. to 9:00 P.M. A luxurious houseboat equipped for up to ten people is available for rent at the marina for adventures on the lake. Call 800–648–LAKE from Washington and British Columbia, and (509) 633–0201 from other areas, for information and reservations.

Visit ⊃**Fort Spokane** to find out what life was like for late-nineteenth-century American soldiers. Built in 1880 after the overt wars against Native Americans were over, Fort Spokane's main function was to maintain a truce between land-hungry settlers and the semi-nomadic Indian tribes. In the twenty years that the fort was active, its deadly force was never used, but patrols, drills, and other military displays were often employed to remind both sides of the army's presence. Now, "frontier regulars" live the garrison life at the fort every other weekend throughout the summer; they dress and eat like the soldiers, sleep in tents, and perform for the public on Sundays.

Fort Spokane is located just off Highway 25, one mile south of the Columbia River. The visitors center has audio and visual displays and is open daily from 9:30 A.M. to 5:30 P.M. The center is located in the former guardhouse, one of the original fort buildings that still stands. An interpretive trail guides you through the grounds and ruins. Surrounded by beautiful forest-covered hills and now-silent reminders of military life, you can imagine the site's transformation from wilderness to fort and back again.

You can continue north on scenic Highway 25 to Kettle Falls (described later in the section on Eastern Rivers and Lakes) or plunge back into rolling grain country by turning south to **Davenport.** This larger agricultural town is very much alive, vibrant with commerce and daily farm life. The Davenport city park, south of the highway, surrounds a natural spring where huge cottonwoods have grown for centuries. The sweet water made this an important campsite for native tribes and, in the late nineteenth century, for settlers and miners traveling along the White Bluffs Road, "the finest trail in the Pacific Northwest." The park is a pleasant spot for a picnic, with playground equipment, tables, shade, and a community pool. Nearby, at Seventh and Park, is the ⊃**Lincoln County Historical Museum**, chock-full of items and images collected over the past century, including photos, farm machinery, a general store, and a blacksmith shop. You'll even find the death mask of outlaw Harry Tracy, killed in Davenport in 1902. For more information, contact the Davenport Chamber of Commerce, Box 869, Davenport 99122; (800) 326–8148.

The rolling landscape continues east along Highway 2. At the town of Reardan you can continue to Spokane or turn north to Colville on Highway 231 for a beautiful drive up Spring Creek Canyon. Along this road you'll see a scattering of old farms, many of which still use windmills to pump water for irrigation. By the time you reach the Spokane River at Long Lake Dam, the wheat fields and farms have given way to ponderosa pine forests and meadows. At the tiny village of Ford you can have your needs met at the **Ford Trading Post,** a post office, general store, rest stop, and gas station all jumbled together in a log building.

Just north of "town" is a granite marker to indicate the site of the Tshimakain Mission. From 1838 to 1848, Reverends Cushing Eells and Elkanah Walker lived and worked at the mission, learning the local Spokane language and teaching tribespeople about farming as well as Christianity. But crop failures, epidemics, the tribe's preference for a hunter-gatherer lifestyle, and the tragic death of colleagues in Walla Walla caused the families to give up and move to safer territory in Oregon.

Continue on Highway 231 as the road curves west through Springdale. Nine miles north at the town of Valley, turn left on a 3-mile spur road to reach **Waitts Lake.** Waitts is a beautiful spring-fed lake surrounded by wetlands and pine forests. Scattered farms and fields dot its western shore, summer cabins and resorts hug the northeast, with public fishing spots at the south end. The resorts are informal, catering to local families as well as visitors. ⊃**Silver Beach Resort** (3323 Waitts Lake Road, Valley 99181; 509–937–2811) is the nicest of the resorts. It has lakeshore cabins, a general store, boat rentals, swimming and picnic sites, and a pleasant restaurant with a patio overlooking the lake (open for dinner Wednesday through Friday, and 8:00 A.M. to 10:00 P.M. on weekends).

Eastern Rivers and Lakes

Spokane, the largest city in the inland Northwest, is located along the Spokane River at an ancient Indian campsite, where members of the Spo-kan-ee tribe (meaning "children of the sun") gathered for centuries to fish at the river rapids. Although Spokane has grown into a major urban center, it retains much of its frontier identity. You'll see plenty of cowboy hats and beat-up pickup trucks even in downtown, and you don't have to go far past the city's suburban developments to find old ranches and farms.

The Spokane River is still a dominant feature in the city. The ⊃**Spokane River Centennial Trail,** which follows the Spokane River, offers visitors an enjoyable way to experience many of the city's best attractions. It's an ideal path for walking, bicycling, running, or skating. The Centennial Trail runs 22 miles from the Idaho border to Spokane's **Riverfront Park** in the center of downtown, where you can still see the churning rapids where the Spokane tribe once caught salmon. This 100-acre park has playgrounds, paths, a train, outdoor theaters, and an arcade as well as the 1909 hand-carved Looff Carousel (open noon to 9:00 P.M. daily in summer, and to 5:00 P.M. on winter weekends). Call the park office at (509) 625–6600 for more information. To find out more about the Centennial Trail, you can stop by or call the Friends of the Centennial Trail office open weekdays from 9:00 A.M. to 4:00 P.M. across the street from Riverfront Park, at 609 West Spokane Falls Boulevard (509–624–3430).

There are other worthwhile places to explore in Spokane. The **Magic Lantern Theater** features foreign and art films at the Atrium, at South 123 Wall (509–838–4919). The **Thai Cafe** (410 West Sprague Avenue; 509–838–4783), hidden away from most downtown foot traffic, is worth finding for its spicy chicken dishes and exotic desserts. **Patsy Clark's Mansion Restaurant** (2208 West Second Avenue; 509–838–8300), is in the city's historic Browne's Addition across from Coeur d'Alene Park. Born in Ireland in 1850, Patrick (Patsy) Clark acquired his wealth in the mining industry in northeast Washington. He became part of Spokane's ultra-elite during the turn-of-the century. Clark commissioned the city's finest architect, Kirtland Cutter, to build his mansion. Before Clark saw any plans, however, he sent Cutter to Europe for inspiration. The restaurant offers elegant dinners and lunches as well as tours of the luxurious mansion. Lunch is served from 11:30 A.M. to 1:30 P.M. weekdays, Sunday brunch is from 10:00 A.M. to 1:30 P.M., and dinner is from 5:00 to 8:30 P.M. Monday through Saturday. The best time to tour the home is just after the doors open at 3:00 P.M. on Saturdays, after Sunday brunch, or in between lunch and dinner on weekdays.

Across the street from Patsy Clark's is **Fotheringham House Victorian Bed and Breakfast,** 2128 West Second Avenue, Spokane 99204; 509–838–4363), located in a house built by the Clark family in 1891 to live in while their grand mansion (Patsy Clark's) was under construction. Present owners Phyllis and Howard Ball maintain the house, with its hand-carved woodwork and tin ceilings, in classic Victorian style. You'll find it a charming base from which to experience the city. The **Waverly Place** bed and breakfast (709 West Waverly Place, Waverly 99205; 509–328–1856), another restored Victorian situated across from a park, features Swedish breakfasts, three elegant rooms, and a wide porch overlooking Corbin Park. Spokane offers many other excellent choices of bed and breakfasts, both Victorian and contemporary, in urban and rural settings. Pat Conly of the Spokane Bed and Breakfast Reservation Service (627 East Twenty-fifth, Waverly 99203; 509–624–3776) can help you choose and arrange your stay at no extra charge.

From Spokane you can take Highway 2 north through lush farmlands to the gentle Pend Oreille (pond-er-RAY) River Valley. On the banks of the Pend Oreille River, you'll find the town of Newport, and its Idaho neighbor, Oldtown. As you enter Newport from the southwest, you'll see **Centennial Plaza** to your right with its huge steam-engine wheel and the ⊃**Pend Oreille County Historical Museum** in the beautiful 1908 brick railroad passenger depot. The museum features antique quilts, kitchen items, books, photographs, tools, and news articles from local sources, as well as a settler's cabin, a one-room schoolhouse, and old farm machinery. It is open daily from 10:00 A.M. to 4:00 P.M. mid-May through September. Call (509) 447–5388 or 447–2770 for information.

Centennial Plaza also has a three-level drinking fountain "serving man, beast, and dog" since 1911. Across the street is Newport's oldest building, **Kelly's Tavern,** a watering hole for miners, loggers, settlers, railway workers, and city folk since 1894. If the walls could talk, what stories they would tell of frontier town dramas! The tavern's impressive lead-glass bar was shipped around the Horn to San Francisco and then carried by wagon train to Newport. A few blocks west at Fourth Street and Cass Avenue is **Burroughs House Bed and Breakfast** (P.O. Box 1822, Newport 99156; 509–447–2590). Built in 1907, this three-story house in a quiet residential neighborhood exudes turn-of-the-century charm with a big front porch, natural wood-finished interiors, handcrafted clocks, and tastefully decorated rooms. Hosts Anne and Gary Burroughs offer light or hearty breakfasts and accommodations for guests (children over 12 only) on weekends.

You can travel north on either side of the Pend Oreille River, but Le Clerc Road on the east bank is more scenic. The reduced traffic on Le Clerc makes it an ideal bicycling route. A half-mile

Steam Engine Wheel in Centennial Plaza

north from the Newport/Oldtown Bridge you can visit an ancient Indian campsite at ⊃**Pioneer Park.** Recent archaeological studies there have uncovered artifacts, earth ovens, and house pits that indicate use by the Kalispel tribe for at least 800 years and by prehistoric hunter-gatherers for possibly 2,000 to 4,000 years. The Salish word Kalispelum means "great camas digging-place," and the Kalispel people cherished the nutritious bulbs of the blue camas flowers that grow wild at this spot and all along the river. The park offers quiet, forested camp and picnic spots, pathways to the river's grassy banks, and views of mergansers, herons, and other waterfowl in nearby wetlands and river islands. For more information contact the Newport District Ranger, P.O. Box 770, Newport 99156; (509) 447–3129.

As you continue north, watch for osprey, a small hawk that catches fish by speed-diving into water and builds large nests on river pilings and snags. The numerous old pilings in shallow water that they prefer were once used to moor the log rafts towed to riverside sawmills. A bridge crosses the river at Usk, a tiny mill town named for a Welsh river, where you can stay at **The Inn at Usk** (north on River Road just west of the bridge, P.O. Box 100, Usk 99180; 509–445-1526). Innkeepers Stan and Andrea Davey strive to re-create the simple rustic ambience of Usk's early days, offering "cozy rooms and friendly people." The **Ponderay Newsprint Company,** 1 mile south of Usk, offers tours of a modern paper mill, weekdays during the summer. Call (509) 445–1511 to schedule a tour.

A few miles north of the Usk bridge on Le Clerc Road, you may spot a herd of buffalo in pastures by the river. This is the **Kalispel Indian Reservation,** the smallest Indian reservation in Washington. The Kalispel people once numbered over a thousand, spread out over the river valley. The tribe was ignored during nineteenth-century treaty negotiations and only received their small land allotment in 1914. Now numbering in the hundreds, the tribe has worked to consolidate their small holdings and have developed community buildings, a bison herd raised for meat, and an aluminum plant in Cusick. You can get a closer look at the tribe's buffalo farm by turning left at the tribal office, on Le Clerc Road next to a small white church, and then left again toward the herd. Call (509) 445–1147 for more information.

The beautiful ⊃**Manresa Grotto** is located a few miles north of the tribal office. A short climb up a winding dirt pathway takes you to the dome-shaped grotto, formed by the waves of an ancient glacial lake. There you'll find rows of stone pews before an altar of mortared rock, site of religious ceremonies for more than a century. The view from the grotto is enchanting—the peaceful river valley surrounded by forested hills, all framed by the gray stone arch of the entrance.

Le Clerc Road ends across the bridge from the town of Ione (eye-OWN). Ione was once the site of the most successful mill in northeast Washington. You can get a historic walking-tour brochure at the Ione Drug Store at Main and Fourth. Just west of the drugstore is the Old Railroad Depot, built in 1909. From the depot you can take in some breathtaking scenery on the historic North Pend Oreille Valley **Lion's Excursion Train** to Metaline Falls and back. Two-hour rides are scheduled around Memorial Day, Fourth of July, Down River Days in late July, Labor Day, and Autumn Colors Weekends in October. Call (509) 442–3397 between noon and 6:00 P.M. for more information and reservations, which must be made at least two weeks before each ride.

For more beautiful scenery, continue northeast on Sullivan Lake Road on the east side of the Pend Oreille River. ᕲ**Sullivan Lake,** dammed in 1910 to run the cement plant at Metaline Falls, is situated at the foot of snow-capped peaks. There are forested campsites at Noisy Creek at the lake's south end and near the Sullivan Lake Ranger District Office at the north end. **Sullivan Lake Trail** connects the two campsites and offers beautiful views, especially during autumn, as well as lakeshore access. The **Mill Pond Historic Site** includes a barrier-free interpretive trail from the western edge of Mill Pond, a small lake created in 1910 and located northwest on Sullivan Lake Road. The path follows a wooden flume that once ran between Sullivan Lake and Metaline Falls. Contact the Sullivan Lake Ranger District, 12641 Sullivan Lake Road, Metaline Falls 99153 (509–446–2691) to find out about other scenic hikes in the area.

Continue west on Sullivan Lake Road to reach **Metaline Falls,** a small town nestled on the east bank of the Pend Oreille River that has attracted a lively artist community. The town's block-long main street (Fifth Street) ends at the city park and visitors center, a brightly painted railway car above terraced flower beds. To the left of the park is the vine-covered ᕲ**Washington Hotel** (P.O. Box 2, Metaline Falls 99153; 509–446–4415). Built in

1910, the hotel has been restored to its earlier elegance as the centerpiece of a bustling turn-of-the-century mining town. Metaline Falls artist and mayor Lee McGowan decorated the eighteen rooms and maintains a delightful gallery, studio, and art study center on the hotel's first floor. Also on the ground floor, you can enjoy delicious baked sweets and a variety of fresh breads at the wonderful family-owned bakery, **Katie's Oven.** The bakery is open Thursday through Sunday, 9:00 A.M. to 4:30 P.M. (509–446–4806).

Down Fifth Street is **The Cutter Theater,** built early in the century and named for talented Spokane architect Kirtland Cutter. The historic school, built of locally kilned bricks, is being renovated as a performing art center. Live music and theater programs are scheduled during summer evenings. You are also welcome to tour this "building-buff's dream" during the day. Write to the North County Theater at P.O. Box 133, Metaline Falls 99153, or call (509) 446–4108, for schedules or to reserve a surprisingly affordable summer weekend package, which includes theater tickets, dinner at Del's in Ione, accommodations at the Washington Hotel, and breakfast at Katie's Oven.

For a spectacular view, follow Highway 31 north about 12 miles, then turn left on the three-quarter-mile access road to **Boundary Vista House.** There you'll have excellent views of Boundary Dam in its steep canyon as well as surrounding mountains. To explore two underground wonders, one natural and one human-made, cross back over the river west of Metaline Falls and take the Boundary Road turnoff to Boundary Dam and Gardner Cave. Along the way you'll see beaver dams in the wetlands next to this beautiful woodland road. Several beaver lodges are visible emerging from ponds that also attract a variety of water birds.

Boundary Road divides in 11½ miles. Take the left fork to reach the 1,055-foot ↺**Gardner Cave** at Crawford State Park. The cave's limestone walls formed from the bodies of ancient sea creatures that settled into ooze on the floor of an ancient ocean 500 million years ago. Groundwater seepage cut away the stone over the past 70 million years, creating the passage with its fantastic patterns. Visitors must be accompanied by a ranger to enter the cave. Tours leave from the parking lot at 10:00 A.M., noon, 2:00 P.M. and 4:00 P.M. and take about an hour. Bring along a light jacket or sweater, since the cave is always cool, and a flashlight. For more information, contact Crawford State Park at (509) 446–4065.

The right fork off Boundary Road snakes down to the base of **Boundary Dam.** There you'll find tunnel openings into the solid limestone hillside that beckon visitors into an underground world. Follow the public access tunnel inside the cliff for views of a gargantuan, human-made cavern with turbines spinning beneath 400 feet of solid rock. Guided tours of the facility are available from 10:00 A.M. to 5:30 P.M., daily from June through September, and Thursday through Monday from October through May. Call (509) 446–3073 for more information.

Colville Pine Forests

Three miles south of Ione at Tiger, Highway 20 turns west from the riverbank and heads over the Selkirk Mountains. Watch for bicyclists along the highway, which is part of Bikecentennial's Transcontinental Bicycling Route. You'll gain respect for these hardy riders as the road climbs and descends through evergreen forests and past a chain of glacial lakes cradled among the peaks. The highway follows the Little Pend Oreille River through the Colville National Forest and past the **Little Pend Oreille Wildlife Area.** Leo, Thomas, Gillette, and Twin Lakes all have campsites with lakeshore access. There are plenty of gravel roads and trails to explore where you can find exquisite beauty and solitude. The **Springboard Trail** from East Gillette Campground offers an easy 2.4-mile loop with interpretive highlights on the area's history and ecology as well as a platform with a view of the lakes. The surrounding forests, lakes, and wetlands are home to elk, white-tailed deer, black bear, blue heron, osprey, and trout. July and August are the best times to enjoy delicious wild huckleberries, gooseberries, and currants. Contact the Colville Ranger District at 755 South Main, Colville 99114, or call (509) 684–4557, for more information.

Beaver Lodge Resort, situated on Lake Gillette at the 3,200-foot level on Tiger Pass, is a great retreat both summer and winter, with miles of hiking or cross-country ski trails nearby. The lodge features rustic wood cabins at the lake's edge, RV hookups, forested or lakeside campsites, laundry, swimming, boat rentals, grocery store, and deli overlooking the lake. Contact proprietors

147

Dick and Sandra Garnett, Little Pend Oreille Lakes, 2430 Highway 20 East, Colville 99114 (509–684–5657).

The forest begins to thin as you continue winding west on Highway 20 and descend into the pastoral Colville River Valley. Colville is a large, bustling town at the junction of highways 395 and 20. Half a mile south of Colville on Highway 395, the ↄ**Roadhouse Restaurant** (509–684–3021) features big helpings of excellent southern cooking for lunch Tuesday through Friday and dinner Tuesday through Saturday served in a restored nineteenth-century farmhouse overlooking the valley. In town follow signs from the highway (Fifth Street) leading two blocks uphill on Wynne Street to reach the **Keller House Museum and Historical Park.** A trail leads up from the museum to the Graves Mountain Fire Lookout at the top of a small hill, where you can enjoy a panoramic view of valley, town, and mountains. The museum, open from June through September, Monday through Saturday, from 10:00 A.M. to 4:00 P.M., and on Sundays from 1:00 to 4:00 P.M., tells the area's story in chronological order from geological, native, and European perspectives. Check at the museum about tours and information on the historical buildings at the site or contact the Stevens County Historical Society, P.O. Box 25, Colville 99114; (509) 684–5968.

The terrain is drier west of Colville. In 9 miles watch for the turnoff south across the railroad tracks to ↄ**My Parent's Estate Bed and Breakfast** (P.O. Box 724, Kettle Falls 99141; 509–738–6220). Innkeepers Al and Bev Parent welcome guests to enjoy their 47-acre estate, the site of a historic mission in the 1870s. The main house, elegantly restored in the 1980s, is surrounded by pastoral views and pleasant woodland trails. **Cafe Italiano** (509–738–6480), in Kettle Falls on Meyer Road, a few blocks south of the highway, is a family restaurant popular with locals and visitors. It serves tasty Italian dinners with a charming continental atmosphere. The restaurant is open daily from 4:00 to 9:00 P.M. Tuesday through Thursday, until 10:00 P.M. Fridays and Saturdays, and until 8:00 P.M. on Sundays.

The original site of **Kettle Falls** is believed to be one of the oldest continuously occupied spots in the Northwest. As long as 9,000 years ago, an ancient tribe known as the Shonitkwa fished the steep falls. Over the centuries Indians established vibrant, permanent communities near the falls that existed until European settlement and exploitation eroded traditional lifestyles.

The actual falls and historic sites are now submerged under Lake Roosevelt. During the early spring drawdown in March or April, remnants of flooded islands and historic towns like **Old Marcus** (located about 5 miles north on Highway 25) are revealed. In some years the water gets low enough to walk through the old streets of Marcus. Call (509) 684–3771 for more information.

You can learn more about the "People of the Falls" at the impressive ꓛ**Kettle Falls Historical Center,** on a spur road north of Highway 20 and 3 miles west of Kettle Falls, just before the bridge over the Columbia River. The center features murals and models for each season of the year, telling the ancient story of tribal life near the falls before the arrival of Europeans. The exhibit and gift shop of local artwork are open from 11:00 A.M. to 5:00 P.M., Wednesday through Sunday, from May 15 through September 15. Contact the Kettle Falls Historical Center, P.O. Box KFHC, Kettle Falls 99141, for more information. Farther along this spur road, you can see **St. Paul's Mission,** a simple log structure originally built in the 1840s and restored almost one hundred years later.

Many family-owned fruit orchards in the area offer berries, cherries, apricots, peaches, pears, apples, and grapes in season from June through September. One of the orchards, ꓛ**Twin Springs Farm,** has been building up their soils using natural methods for over twenty years and is a Washington State certified organic farm, producing tomatoes, strawberries, and orchard fruit without the use of pesticides, herbicides, or inorganic fertilizers. Located on a bench of land overlooking the Columbia River a few miles south of Highway 20, the farm is a peaceful spot to pick fruit and admire the view. Be sure to contact the farm first to schedule a visit and find out what's in season. Write to 1744 Heidegger Road, Rice 99167, or call (509) 738–2095. You can also write to the Kettle Falls Chamber of Commerce, P.O. Box 119, Kettle Falls 99141, or call (509) 738–2300, for an orchard directory and map of over a dozen other delightful fruit-picking spots.

Northern Hills and Towns

From the Columbia River, head southwest through Colville National Forest on Highway 20. Watch for the East Portal Picnic Area in about 10 miles where you can stop to explore the **Log**

Flume Trail, a thirty-minute, well-signed walk that details how the area was logged in the 1920s. West of this point the highway has been designated the ⊃**Sherman Pass Scenic Byway** and follows lively Sherman Creek as it cascades from waterfalls near Sherman Pass. Here the road crosses the **Kettle Crest Trail,** which runs 28 miles north and 14 miles south of the byway through rugged mountains and steep talus slopes above the Columbia River. A roadside Forest Service interpretive kiosk a few miles west of the pass describes the devastating White Mountain Fire, started by lightning one hot August afternoon in 1988. Spread by dry winds, it took a month for firefighters to contain the blaze. You can now see the forest's gradual return amidst the standing burnt timber. Contact the Kettle Falls Ranger District, at 255 West Eleventh, Kettle Falls 99141 (509–738–6111), from 7:30 A.M. to 4:00 P.M. weekdays, to find out more about trails and camping along this route.

The **Tin-Na-Tit-Kin-Ne-Ki Art Gallery,** at the 312-mile marker on your left, offers an eclectic display of Indian art from the Northwest coast Haida to the Southwest desert Hopi, from nineteenth-century to contemporary native artists. The gallery is open from 8:00 A.M. to 6:30 P.M. daily, April 1 to November 15; 9:00 A.M. to 5:00 P.M. November 16 to December 23; and by appointment January through March. Write to Ot-Ne-We or Jim Swayne at P.O. Box 1057, Republic 99166, or call (509) 775–3077, for more information.

Bicyclists on the Bikecentennial Transcontinental Route make a beeline for the ⊃**Triangle J Ranch Hostel and Bed and Breakfast** (423 Old Kettle Falls Road, Republic 99166; 509–775–3933), making this a fun place to meet fellow travelers. In summer the fields next to the ranch gardens and stables are often dotted with colorful tents and bicycles. You don't have to be saddle sore to appreciate the warm hospitality of this friendly mountain home. The ranch has private rooms for bed and breakfast guests as well as a four-bed dormitory with cooking facilities, a hot tub, and outdoor swimming pool. To get there, turn right (north) on Highway 21 toward Curlew. In one mile turn right again at Cooke Mountain Road and watch for the sign in ¼ mile.

A loop around **Curlew Lake** to the north makes a pleasant bike ride or drive. The 7-mile-long lake is surrounded by mountains and rolling hills. Curlew Lake was home to Native American

Kettle River History Club's Auto-Truck Museum

settlements long before homesteaders arrived. Some early log cabins are still visible in the area. **Curlew Lake State Park** offers lakeside picnic sites, swimming area, boat launches, and campsites. Several small lakeside resorts are scattered along the lake. **Pine Point Resort** (1060 Pine Point Road, Republic 99166; 509–775–3643) offers fully equipped waterfront cottages and cabins for two to six people and canoe, motorboat and paddleboat rentals, moorage, a fishing pier, grocery store, a sandy beach to swim from, outdoor game equipment, and laundry facilities. A little farther north, **Fisherman's Cove** (1157 Fisherman's Cove Road, Republic 99166; 509–775–3641) welcomes families and offers rustic cabins in a quiet, lakeside setting. **Tiffany's** (1026 Tiffany Road, Republic 99166; 509–775–3152), on the opposite shore, offers amenities comparable to Pine Point Resort.

The Kettle River History Club's **Auto-Truck Museum** is located on Highway 21 between the towns of Malo and Curlew. This is an old-car aficionado's dream: dozens of carefully preserved and restored cars including vintage Model T Fords, Buicks, actor Walter Brennan's 1928 Phaeton, the only 1917 Chevrolet Royal Mail Roadster still running, and one of three 1920 Howard Cooper Firetrucks ever made, all in operating condition. The museum is open from 1:00 to 5:00 P.M. daily in summer. Write to the Kettle River History Club at P.O. Box 96, Curlew 99118, or call Stott's Construction at (509) 779–4987, for more information and to confirm hours.

The quiet town of ⊃**Curlew** is nestled between dry hills on the east bank of the Kettle River. Follow signs to the right off the highway, then left and right again into town. Curlew's main street, lined with dark-wood buildings with Western false fronts, overlooks the river through tall cottonwoods. The old **Ansorage Hotel and Cafe** no longer provides food or lodging, but you can tour the inn building, which is complete with period furnishings and clothing from its heyday in the early part of this century (weekends from mid-May to the end of September, 1:00 to 5:00 P.M.). Luella Burns, Gladys and Richard Lembcke, and other members of the Kettle River History Club delight in leading visitors back into another time. Call Gladys Lembcke at (509) 779–4955 for more information or to arrange a tour during the week. The **Riverside Bar and Grill,** at 813 River Street (509–779–4813) is so popular it attracts people from all over the region. The restaurant offers Mexican and American food prepared simply from fresh ingredients. The dining room, with its wood-burning stove, fans, and rustic wood furniture, provides a comfortable atmosphere overlooking the river. Dinner is served from 4:00 to 9:00 P.M. Wednesday through Sunday, with prime rib featured Friday through Sunday.

On your way back south on Highway 21 toward Republic, take the West Curlew Lake Road turnoff to your right (west) at Curlew Lake's north end for a less-traveled route along the lake's western shore. Klondike Road veers right about a mile south of the lake and then descends past pine trees and houses hugging the steep hillside into Republic. At the north end of town, you'll pass a lovely stone Episcopal church, built in 1909, whose windows shimmer with stained-glass doves. A narrow valley cut by two parallel streets and alleys running north and south constitutes downtown.

Clark Avenue, the main road through town, was named for Republic Gold Mining and Milling Company president "Patsy" Clark (whose mansions now serve as a bed and breakfast and an elegant restaurant in Spokane's historic Browne's Addition). While most buildings' false fronts are recent additions to boost the town's already rustic feel, the **Republic Drug Store** (circa 1906), on the corner of Clark and Fourth Avenues, boasts an original storefront with hand-cranked awnings and pressed tin ceiling still in great condition. Up Clark Avenue, **Anderson Grocery** has offered general merchandise since 1900, while the **Ferry County Co-op** provides for the modern homesteading community.

To participate in an archaeological treasure hunt, follow Sixth Avenue west a block onto Kean Street across from Patterson Park to the Ɔ**Stonerose Interpretive Center,** open May through October, Tuesday through Saturday, from 10:00 A.M. to 5:00 P.M. There, curator Lisa Barksdale and her assistants can introduce you to the fascinating world of 50 million years ago, when an ancient lake covered the town site of Republic. More than 200 plant species, a third of them now extinct, settled in the lake bed during the Eocene Epoch, leaving impressions in the mud that now provide paper-thin "windows" onto prehuman history. The small center, named for the Republic fossil of the oldest known ancestor of the rose family, has several examples of local plant and fish fossils as well as a sandbox in which both children and adults can search through stones to find their own imprints of ancient plants. Guided-fossil hunting tours leave from the center at 10:00 A.M. and 2:00 P.M. Bring along a hammer and chisel, or rent some there, to use at the dig site north of town. The fossils you discover will be identified for you to take home or, if you are lucky enough to find a new or rare species, you will be applauded as an archaeological hero and your fossil will be kept for further study. Scientists of national and international renown continue to explore and investigate specimens found at the site. The center has educational materials for sale and offers memberships to those who would like to support this organization. Contact Stonerose Interpretive Center at P.O. Box 987, Republic 99166, or call (509) 775–2295.

Off the Beaten Path in Southeast Washington

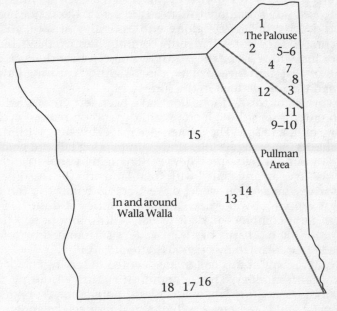

1. The Palouse
2. 5–6
4. 7
8
12. 3
11
9–10

Pullman Area

15

In and around Walla Walla

13 14

18 17 16

Southeast Washington

Southeast Washington is a region of sensuous, rolling hills and giant blue skies. Much of the land is covered with waving fields of dry-land (unirrigated) wheat. This landscape offers endless variations of shapes, textures, and colors that are always interesting. The best way to explore this area is to get off the major highways and drive or bicycle along endless miles of farm roads connecting the area's small, friendly communities. Walking, bicycling, or just sitting along the roadside, you can hear the melodious trill of a western meadowlark, catch sight of a soaring hawk, and smell the soil warmed in the sun.

Few corners of this fertile region have been left untouched by human enterprise, although crops still depend on natural cycles of snow, rain, and sun. The immense acreage, bursting with new green shoots following spring rains or undulating tall and golden in the late summer sun, provides ever-changing visual splendor. Residents' lives are integrated with their land and the seasons. In early spring, huge eight-wheel-drive tractors comb the terrain pulling twenty-foot-wide plows that raise spires of dust. In late summer giant combines harvest wheat, lentils, and peas. Farmhouses and big old barns nestle in valleys surrounded by a few tall shade trees planted by previous generations.

The quiet towns of this region are devoted to serving the hardworking farm families. These communities thrived during the first half of the century when larger local populations supported more social and commercial activities and farmers depended on rail transport to ship crops to market. Walking down any main street, you'll see beautiful old brick buildings that once housed banks, stores, and fraternal organizations, many now empty, and huge grain elevators next to rail depots.

These communities welcome visitors. Stop at the local cafe (many towns have only one) where, for the price of a cup of coffee or a piece of homemade pie, you can receive a lesson in local history and gossip from fellow patrons eager to swap stories. The town cemetery, usually located on a nearby picturesque hilltop, is also a good place to learn about the community's past by noting headstone names and dates.

The Palouse

Palouse is derived from the French word "pelouse," meaning green lawn, an appropriate name for one of the most fertile grain-growing regions in the world. Equestrians may be interested to know that the Appaloosa, a breed of horses distinguished by its spotted coat and gentle disposition, are descendants of animals that were used by the native people of the Palouse.

Although most of this region is now farmed, there are still areas where the original Palouse environment is preserved. Chief of these is the ⊃**Turnbull National Wildlife Refuge,** south of Spokane on the Cheney-Plaza road. The refuge includes miles of lakes and marshes that attract a wide variety of wildlife. Generations before pioneers arrived the Spokane tribe cherished this natural garden for its abundant roots and herbs such as camas, wild onion, and kinnikinnick. Migrating and nesting water birds thrive in the rich wetlands on which they increasingly depend as more land is cultivated and developed.

Early farmers tried to drain these "swamps" but found the soil poor. Rescued from development in the 1920s, the area was set aside as a wildlife preserve in 1937. Now visitors to Turnbull can bicycle, walk, or drive on a 5-mile gravel loop road to experience the area's original beauty. Signs along the Pine Creek Trail help acquaint you with the area's background and natural history. A wooden boardwalk over shallow Black Horse Lake allows close-up viewing of this wetland and the dabbler ducks that live there. Nearby, deeper 30 Acre Lake attracts diving ducks such as canvasbacks, scaups, and ruddy ducks. Equipped with field glasses you may see colorful, tree-nesting wood ducks or reclusive hooded mergansers. For more information contact the Refuge Manager at Turnbull NWR, South 26010 Smith Road, Cheney 99004; (509) 235–4723.

Heading south on Rock Lake Road, watch the landscape change from rocky pine-covered meadows to rolling wheat farms. The terrain changes again around ⊃**Rock Lake,** a quiet expanse of water surrounded by basalt outcroppings. This area was the home of Chief Kamiaken of the Yakima Indian Nation. Kamiaken was banished after the Indian War of 1855 and lived around Rock Lake until his death in 1877. Local residents believe that the lake is inhabited by a giant serpent, perhaps a long-lived dinosaur or a cousin of the Loch Ness monster, so be watchful. Along the lake's southeast shore you can see the **Milwaukee Road Corridor,** a railroad line until 1980 and now converted to a public trail. This is part of a trail system stretching from King County to the Idaho border that is used by hikers, bicyclists, equestrians, and even wagon trains. Such trails are a wonderful way to experience the environment, removed from the impacts of motor traffic. Maps showing access points, and permits to use the trail, required along this stretch, are available from the Washington Department of Natural Resources at 713 Bowers Road, Ellensburg 98926–9341 (509–925–6131).

After traveling through the rolling hills of the Palouse, you will enjoy seeing the region from a different perspective. There are two towering buttes that offer you a chance to look down at the quilted landscape. ⊃**Kamiak Butte County Park,** named for Chief Kamiaken, is an island of pine forest surrounded by wheat fields located 5 miles southwest of the town of Palouse near the Idaho border. The trees offer cool summer shade for picnickers and campers. The 3½-mile Pine Ridge Trail through the forest takes you on a self-guided nature walk to the top of the butte and back. The diverse plant and animal life along the way and the magnificent views from the top make this a rewarding hike. The park has picnic and camping facilities as well as an amphitheater for evening programs on local and natural history (beginning at 8:30 P.M., from late June through August). A special "Lunch On Top" program introduces elementary school age children to the flora, fauna, and geology of the area through enjoyable daylong programs in June and July. Write to Whitman County Parks, Fair and Developmental Services, U.S. Bank Building, Room 3, Colfax 99111, or call (509) 397–6238, for more information or to reserve a space for your child.

⊃**Steptoe Butte,** 15 miles north of Colfax, is a pyramid of granite rising from the gentle landscape, crowned with radio antennas. The smaller hills and mountains that once surrounded this and Kamiak buttes were washed away by gigantic lava flows ten to thirty million years ago. The low, fertile soils that now surround these buttes formed during the Ice Age when wind-blown deposits (loess) buried the landscape up to 200 feet thick. A two-story hotel stood at the top of Steptoe Butte from 1888 until 1911, when it burned in a spectacular fire that could be seen throughout the Palouse region. Although views from the rooftop balcony were excellent, the hotel never attracted the crowds of tourists that developer James Davis had hoped for, and it was plagued with water supply problems. Steptoe's summit is easily accessible by a road that circles around the butte. At the top you'll find displays explaining the Palouse geology and a magnificent 360-degree panorama that stretches practically forever. Although the treeless summit is stark, there are pleasant picnic sites in the wooded areas at the base of the butte.

North of Steptoe Butte in the town of Oakesdale, you can spend a night at the ⊃**Hanford Castle Bed and Breakfast** (P.O. Box 23, Oakesdale 99158; 509–285–4120). This charming Victorian mansion perches on a hilltop overlooking Oakesdale and many miles of wheat-covered hills. Views from the mansion's turret give a wonderful bird's-eye perspective of the undulating landscape. Castle owners Terri Gravelle and Paul Mathews are renovating this historic building with great care and attention to detail. They welcome visitors to tour their seventeen-room mansion, which features elegant hand-carved wooden banisters, brown marble washbasins, claw-foot tubs, art glass windows, fireplaces adorned with imported tiles and mirrors, and an indoor garden. Reservations are recommended for tours and accommodations.

Oakesdale is also home to ⊃**Joseph's Flour,** at 103 East Jackson (509–285–4652), a small processor of high-quality organic grain flour. Joseph Barron grinds wheat and corn in a small but efficient mill in his own garage. His freshly ground, top-quality products are available for sale there, and with customers willing to visit he makes no effort to sell his flour through commercial distributors. He delights in demonstrating his operation to customers and visitors. You might not have considered flour milling to be a high art until you see the care and specialized knowledge that Barron puts into his grain products. Joseph's father, J.C. Barron, owned and ran the Oakesdale flour mill starting in 1907, and Joseph spent most of his long life in various mill jobs.

The family's original flour mill still stands across a creek from the small shed where Joseph's Flour is now produced. Barron sometimes gives tours, and the mill is open to the public the last weekend in May during the town's Old Mill Days celebration. If you have the opportunity to see inside, don't miss it. The huge timber frame structure, which was moved piece by piece from

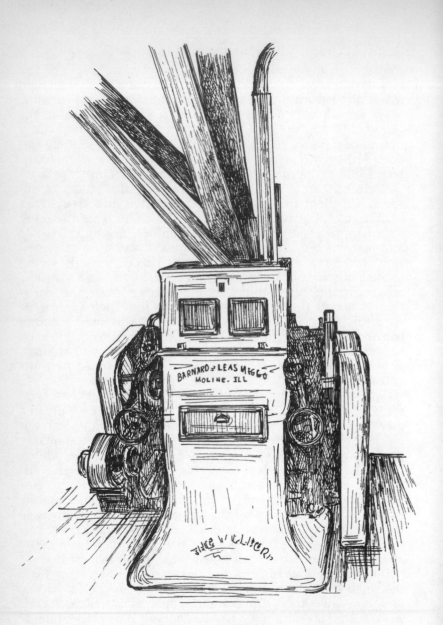

Barron's Mill

Illinois in 1889, still contains the original milling and sifting equipment, which dates from the nineteenth century. Grain descended a labyrinth of perfectly fitted wooden chutes through various processes on each of the building's four stories to finish as flour on the ground floor. You can easily imagine what the now-silent mill must have been like during its busy years, when a central steam engine drove the complex network of belts and shafts powering conveyers, grinders, and sifters. The mill was used to produce flour until 1939 and continued as a grain cleaning and storage facility until the 1960s. The old mill is well preserved and tidy, ready to help feed the world once again if called on.

The つ**McCroskey House** (P.O. Box 95, Garfield 99130; 509–635–1459), along Highway 27 on the north side of the town of Garfield, is another charming Victorian-era mansion now serving as a bed and breakfast guest house. Owners Nick and Donna Manring are renovating their home to its original character, including a wood-burning kitchen stove used for household cooking and the restoration of beautiful murals that graced the spacious dining room. Garfield is a pleasant town. The Manrings, both of whom have families that have lived in the community for generations, can supply guests with many suggestions for things to see and do in the area.

Bishop's U-Pick Orchard (509–635–1276), in Garfield at Eighth and Adams Street (follow paved Spokane Street west past Garfield's city park until you see Bishop's nine-acre orchard, house, and cider shed), offers a wealth of apples from mid-September through the end of October. You'll find Sally and Steven Bishop's orchard as delightful in springtime, overflowing with apple blossoms, as it is delicious at harvest time. People come from miles around to make their own fresh juice on Steven Bishop's four handmade oak cider presses, patterned after the ones his great-grandfather used when he homesteaded in Garfield.

South of Garfield is the quiet town of Palouse, once a bustling commercial center supplying gold mining and logging camps in Idaho. The town's main street is lined with beautiful brick buildings, many now silent and unused. Palouse's Main Street historic district is listed on the National Register of Historic Places. One old storefront now houses the つ**Boomerang Newspaper Museum,** at 110 East Main Street, where you can see old presses and other printing equipment. Museum hours are limited, but visitors can arrange access by calling (509) 878–1309 or the Whitman County Tourist Information at (800) 562–4570.

Pullman Area

Residents of Pullman don't consider their city off the beaten path. Pullman is the Palouse region's largest city and a bustling mixture of agricultural businesses and student life. It is home to Washington State University (WSU, pronounced Wazoo), which emphasizes agricultural sciences. The Pullman Chamber of Commerce (North 415 Grand Avenue, Pullman 99163; 509–334–3565) offers a walking-tour brochure that leads you around the college and Pioneer Hill districts, where many buildings date from the turn of the century.

The ⊃**Kimbrough House** Bed and Breakfast (505 Maiden Lane, Pullman 99163; 509–334–3866) is an excellent example of this period and a wonderful place to spend a night. Owner Marcia Kammerzell maintains the 1916 house in its original style. There are five guest rooms, two with private baths, two sun porches, and a warm fireplace to welcome guests on cool evenings. Breakfasts are as hearty or as light as you choose. High tea, featuring scones, light sandwiches, fruit, desserts, and lots of tea, offered Wednesdays from 4:00 to 6:00 P.M. is a specialty of the house. There are plenty of places to shop and eat in Pullman. If you want to splurge, enjoy dinner at **Seasons Restaurant,** on Paradise Street just east of Grand Avenue, which offers sumptuous, elegant meals and a hilltop view. The restaurant (509–334–1410) is open 5:30 to 9:00 P.M., Tuesday through Saturday.

WSU has a splendid **Museum of Anthropology** featuring displays on human evolution and on the development of language and culture—and on the Northwest's mysterious Sasquatch. The museum is open weekdays during the school year (Monday to Thursday from 9:00 A.M. to 4:00 P.M., Fridays from 9:00 A.M. to 3:00 P.M.). Tours can be scheduled two weeks in advance by calling (509) 335–3441. Art lovers can enjoy the University's **Museum of Art,** in the Fine Arts Building at the corner of Stadium Way and Farm Way. The gallery offers eleven changing exhibitions a year, featuring past and contemporary international, regional, and student artists working in painting, sculpture, photography, and architecture. There is something for every taste. The gallery is open on Thursdays from 10:00 A.M. to 4:00 P.M. and from 7:00 to 10:00 P.M., on Fridays from 10:00 A.M. to 4:00 P.M., and on weekends from 1:00 to 5:00 P.M.

After you've worked up an appetite from museum touring, you'll want to stop at ↄ**Ferdinands,** a campus ice cream parlor named after the pacifist, flower-sniffing bull. On the walls are quotations by author Munro Leaf and illustrations by Robert Lawson from the classic book about Ferdinand beloved by generations of children. Ferdinands sells WSU's own Cougar brand of high-quality dairy products (including gourmet cheeses), produced by the Departments of Food Science and Human Nutrition of the College of Agriculture and Home Economics. Ferdinands is located behind the Human Nutrition building, next to the tennis courts on South Fairway Road. Its hours are 9:30 A.M. to 4:30 P.M. weekdays.

For a step back in time to the Old West, visit the ↄ**Three Forks Pioneer Village Museum,** located about 4 miles north of Pullman. This re-created town, assembled during the past three decades by farmer Roger Rossebo, has a general store, barber shop, blacksmith's shop, jail, and hardware store, displaying thousands of antiques dating from the 1800s, including a piano shipped around Cape Horn, a pioneer kitchen, and a schoolhouse. The museum is open most Sundays, from 1:00 to 5:00 P.M., and other days by appointment from May to September. There is a small fee. Call (509) 332–3889 for reservations and directions.

Colfax is the Whitman County seat and a prosperous commercial center along the banks of the Palouse River. The ↄ**Perkins House** (623 North Perkins Street; turn west on Last Street and follow the sign at the end of the street) is a magnificent mansion listed on the National Register of Historic Places. It was built in 1884 by James Perkins, an early settler who established his fortune by constructing the region's first sawmill. It is open for tours from 1:00 to 5:00 P.M., Thursdays and Sundays, from June to August. An old-fashioned ice cream social held at the mansion the last Sunday in June is a major annual event. For more information, contact the Colfax Chamber of Commerce, P.O. Box 166, Colfax 94111–0166; 509–397–3712. The **Tulin House** bed and breakfast, located on a hillside at South 812 Main Street, Colfax 99111 (509–397–3312), is a cheery Victorian home with Tiffany windows, period furnishings, and down comforters.

South of Pullman at the confluence of the Snake and Clearwater rivers, you can visit **Clarkston** (once called Jawbone Flat) and, across the Snake River, **Lewiston**, Idaho. These twin cities are the embarking point for adventures at Hells Gate State Park, the Nez Perce Reservation, and boat or raft tours through Hells Canyon, the deepest river gorge in the United States. Contact the Clarkston Chamber of Commerce at (800) 933–2128 or (509) 758–7712 for information on river trips. You'll find extensive bike paths, parks, and historical information on the levees that line both sides of the river. The 6-mile path from Clarkston, past the towering basalt cliffs of Swallows Park, to the county seat of **Asotin** is ideal for family bicycling. While in Asotin you can stop by the **Asotin County Historical Museum** and enjoy a pleasant lunch in town.

In and around Walla Walla

The town of **Dayton** is another historic and charming community in southeast Washington. When Lewis and Clark explored the region on their return trip in 1806, what is now Dayton's main street served as a racetrack for native tribes who camped in the area. First homesteaded by cattle ranchers in 1859, grain farming took over within a few years. Dayton was chosen as a stagecoach stop between Walla Walla and Lewiston. Logs from the Blue Mountains were once delivered to the town for milling into lumber by an 18-mile flume. By 1880 Dayton had become the Columbia County seat and was an industrious community with mills, a brewery, newspapers, seven churches, and an impressive courthouse surrounded by elegant homes.

A good place to begin your tour is at the ↄ**Dayton Depot,** the oldest existing railway station in the state. To get there, turn west from Main Street onto Commercial. The depot is open from 1:00 to 4:00 P.M., Tuesday through Saturday, from June through August, and Tuesday through Friday from September through May. Pick up a brochure describing the town's rich architectural history, including extensive details on many pioneer cottages and elegant turn-of-the-century homes. Wear comfortable shoes so you can enjoy the self-guided walking tours. For more information call the Dayton Chamber of Commerce at (509) 382–4825 or write the Dayton Historical Depot Society, P.O. Box 1881, Dayton 99328.

The **Purple House Bed and Breakfast** (415 East Clay Street, Dayton 99328; 509–382–3159), built in 1882 by a pioneer physician and philanthropist, is one of Dayton's finest homes and one of the town's several bed and breakfast options. Present owner D. Christine Williscroft has preserved the house's gracious past while adding her own European flair. Williscroft offers delicious meals, two charming rooms, a serene library, and beautifully decorated parlor as well as a heated outdoor pool and Jacuzzi.

If walking makes you thirsty, stop at the **Elk Drug Store,** at 271 Main Street, to sample from an old-fashioned soda fountain. For a gourmet meal in an elegant setting, reserve your spot early at the popular Ꙩ**Patit Creek Restaurant,** which claims to be the only four-star restaurant in the region. It's at 725 East Dayton Avenue, on Highway 12 at the north end of town (509–382–2625). Patit Creek serves lunch and dinner Tuesday through Friday and dinner on Saturdays. If you can't get reservations at this charming spot, try the **Sicilian Cafe** (509–382–3035) at 176½ Main Street in downtown Dayton for a tasty Italian meal. The owner of the cafe grew up in New York in a similar cafe run by her grandparents so you know the cooking is authentic. The restaurant is open from 6:30 A.M. to 8:00 P.M. Monday through Wednesday, 6:30 A.M. to 9:00 P.M. Thursday through Saturday, and from 6:30 A.M. to 7:00 P.M. on Sunday.

Dayton is the access point for the beautiful Blue Mountains in the Umatilla National Forest, which includes the spectacular 177,412-acre Wenaha-Tucannon Wilderness, an area of steep ridges, talus slopes, and tablelands accessible only by trail. Wildlife includes Rocky Mountain elk, white-tailed and mule deer, bighorn sheep, black bear, cougar, bobcat, and many species of birds. It's also a popular area for mushroom picking. For information call the Pomeroy Ranger Station at (509) 843–1891. During the winter you may enjoy **Ski Bluewood,** one of the few large downhill ski resorts in southeast Washington, in the Blue Mountains 22 miles southeast of Dayton. Its Skyline Express chair provides a vertical rise of 1,125 feet and 26 downhill runs. A Triple Nickel chairlift is appropriate for beginning and intermediate skiers. Call (509) 382–4725 for information.

ꙨPalouse Falls**, 38 miles north of Dayton on Highway 261 is a spectacular waterfall offering a glimpse of what the many river canyons (called coulees) in the area looked like before most were dammed. The falls tumble hundreds of feet over basalt-column cliffs, surrounded by grass- and sage-covered hills. The park offers breathtaking views, and picnic and camping sites. The terrain is especially striking in spring when new grass colors the hills with green, wildflowers sprout along the paths, and fresh sage scents the air.

To the south, Walla Walla Valley, called "The Place of the People of the Rye Grass" by the Cayuse tribe, is still known primarily for fertile fields of grain, now mainly wheat. **Walla Walla** is a quiet farm and college town nestled in the heart of the valley. Whitman College, near downtown, has a pleasant, tree-covered campus that deserves a walk, and a number of nineteenth-century mansions scattered around make the nearby neighborhoods fun to explore.

There are two very charming guest homes in Walla Walla. The 1909 **Green Gables Inn** (922 Bonsella, Walla Walla 99362; 509–525–5501) has served as a family home, a residence for nurses, and most recently has been beautifully renovated as a bed and breakfast by Jim and Margaret Buchan with plenty of hand work and period antiques. Each of the five guest rooms has a name (Mayflowers, Idlewild, Willomere, Dryad's Bubble, and Birchpath, which are all from the book *Anne of Green Gables*) and a unique personality. Each room has a private bath, and two have private outside decks. The elegant three-story **Stone Creek Inn** (720 Bryant Avenue, Walla Walla 99362; 509–529–8120) was built in 1883 by Miles C. Moore, a successful merchant and the last territorial governor. Two tastefully furnished guest rooms allow visitors to share in the splendor of the past century.

For something a little different you may want to visit or stay at the ↄ**Sicyon** (1283 Star Street, Walla Walla 99362; 509–525–2964), a bed and breakfast guest home combined with an art gallery, all located on the ground floor of a renovated 1885 carriage house. The single guest room and private bath are adjacent to the gallery displays, and breakfast is served in the gallery itself. The gallery features a variety of traditional and contemporary Northwest fine arts, including the work of Sicyon owner Bill Piper, who in addition to running the gallery and the bed and breakfast is a full-time art instructor at Whitman College. Located half a mile from the college and 1 mile from downtown, Sicyon is a perfect base for exploring Walla Walla by foot or bicycle. Piper even offers to pick up visitors from the airport or bus station in his stylish 1950 Dodge. Reservations are recommended.

Southwest of town is the ⊃**Fort Walla Walla Museum Complex,** on the grounds of Fort Walla Walla Park (take Rose Street west from downtown, then turn left on Myra Road). The museum complex includes a re-created pioneer village with fourteen historic log buildings filled with antique household items and settlers' tools. There are also six large museum buildings with additional displays of pioneer life, equipment from horse-farming days, and railroad equipment. There is even a display of historic prison conditions, with a turn-of-the-century prison cell created by Walla Walla Prison's retired warden. These displays were developed and are maintained by Walla Walla Historical Society volunteers.

A full-size mule team combine wheat harvester built in 1919 fills building 3, complete with 33 fiberglass mules attached to a "Shandoney" hitch. This elaborate rig is a reminder of the challenges farmers faced before tractors replaced animal power, and is a sharp contrast to the powerful, air-conditioned equipment now used in the region. Some old-timer museum volunteers can describe from personal experience what it was like to use horse- and mule-drawn equipment to harvest the huge wheat fields that cover the region's rolling landscape. The historical complex is open from 10:00 A.M. to 5:00 P.M., Tuesday through Sunday, from May through September, and on weekends in October. There is a small admission charge, which supports museum development. For information write to the Walla Walla Valley Pioneer and Historical Society at RFD 8, Box 32-B, Walla Walla 99362, or call (509) 525–7703.

If you visit Walla Walla on Mother's Day weekend, you can enjoy seeing 50 passenger balloons flying from Howard Tietan Park at the south end of town. The **Walla Walla Balloon Stampede,** held since 1974, has something for everybody, including sports events, arts and crafts booths, food, and nonstop entertainment. The colorful balloons lift off from the park each morning at dawn and early Saturday evening. Later Saturday night, after the balloons return and darkness falls, the tethered balloons are inflated for the spectacular "Nite Glow" against the starlit sky. There are also volkswalks, runs, art exhibits, pet shows, antique car and motorcycle parades, golf, dancing, and music. The Walla Walla Stampede is the largest annual balloon event in the Pacific Northwest. For additional information contact the Walla Walla Chamber of Commerce at P.O. Box 644, Walla Walla 99362; (800) 743–9562 or (509) 525–0850.

Five miles west of town is the ⊃**Whitman Mission National Historic Site,** which commemorates the mission established there by Marcus and Narcissa Whitman. Museum displays and an interpretive trail on the mission grounds describe the history of the region and bring to life activities in the Walla Walla Valley between 1836 and 1847 when waves of settlers stopped at the mission on their trek along the Oregon Trail. Crossing the Blue Mountains into what is now Washington was one of the last major challenges of the journey west. After traveling more than a thousand miles of dirt roads and rough mountain trails, the settlers found rest and care at Whitman Mission. The fertile Walla Walla Valley, then being tilled by white farmers for the first time, must have looked wonderful after months of difficult travel. But the large influx of settlers and the devastating epidemics they spread to native people created conflicts with the local Cayuse tribe, resulting in the missionaries' tragic deaths. The visitors center is open daily from 8:00 A.M. to 6:00 P.M. in the summer and 8:00 A.M. to 4:30 P.M. in winter. For more information call (509) 522–6360.

Useful Resources

Government Agency Resources

National Park Service
Outdoor Recreation Information, 1018 First Avenue, Seattle 98104, (206) 442–0170. Publications and brochures are available for many national parks and historic sites in Washington.

Washington State Parks and Recreation Commission
Cleanwater Lane, KY-11, Olympia 98504, (206) 753–2027. Numerous publications are available describing the state's extensive parks and recreation activities.

Washington Tourist Information
101 General Administration Building, AX-13, Olympia 98504
Call (800) 544–1800 to request a Washington Travel Kit that includes the Washington State Traveler's Guide. For more specific information, call either (206) 586–2088 or 586–2102 to talk with a volunteer travel counselor who can provide you with brochures and advice to meet your needs and interests.

Washington State Recreation Guide
Interagency Committee for Outdoor Recreation
Available in bookstores or from Publishing Enterprises Inc., P.O. Box 84505, Seattle 98124
This inexpensive (currently $4.95 plus tax and shipping) guide describes hundreds of local, state, and federal recreation sites in Washington.

Washington State Trails Directory
Interagency Committee for Outdoor Recreation
4800 Capitol Boulevard, Tumwater 98504, (206) 753-7140
This free directory lists public hiking, biking, skiing, and equestrian trails in Washington state. Other recreation information is also available.

Other Resources

"Artguide Northwest"
Tiption Publishing Company
13205 Ninth Avenue NW, 98177,
(206) 367–6831
This semiannual pocket guide lists galleries in over a dozen communities in western Washington, providing descriptions of current shows.

"Exploring Washington's Past; A Road Guide To History"
Ruth Kirk and Carmela Alexander
University of Washington Press, Seattle, 1989
This comprehensive handbook describes local history for much of Washington, including fascinating stories and insights about many of the places described in *Washington: Off the Beaten Path*.

"Plants and Animals of the Pacific Northwest"
Eugene Kozloff
University of Washington Press, Seattle, 1976
This interesting and informative guide is the ideal companion for amateur naturalists.

Resource Institute
6532 Phinney Avenue, Seattle 98103, (206) 784–6762
The institute is a nonprofit organization offering environmental education programs on a 65-foot schooner sailing through Puget Sound and the San Juan Islands.

Washington Atlas & Gazeteer
DeLorme Publishing
This atlas provides topographical maps covering all of Washington state at approximately half an inch to the mile, making it ideal for exploring back roads.

Washington Coastweeks
1325 West Bay Drive NW, Olympia 98502, (206) 943–3642
The annual Coastweeks includes dozens of public events around Washington's waterways. Contact this office for a calendar of events.

Washington State Bed and Breakfast Directory
Washington Bed and Breakfast Guild
2442 NW Market Street, Seattle 98107, (509) 548–6224
Over 100 bed and breakfast guest homes are listed in this free brochure.

Washington Outfitters and Guides Association
c/o High Country Outfitters
22845 NE Eighth, #331, Redmond 98053, (206) 392-0111
This organization can help find a professional guide to take you mountain horseback riding, fishing, wilderness hiking, or even on a wagon train ride.

INDEX

173

Index

Index

Index

180